Thou Shalt Not Bear False Witness:

The Truth Behind the Vatican and the Birth of Islam

Thou Shalt Not Bear False Witness:

The Truth Behind the Vatican and the Birth of Islam

* * *

Gary Dale Cearley

* * *

Aux Arcs Publications
2006

*I dedicate this book to the beloved memories of
Cheryl Ann McDonald, Jason Scott Green, Michael David
Smith, Billy Bob Smith and Billy Ray Cearley.*

I know that we will meet again someday...

Contents

Preface

I would just like to take a little bit of time to explain a few things about this text. First of all, you might find in some proper names of people and places that don't correspond directly throughout the entire book. This will occur especially when using foreign terms, and once again especially Arabic. I have tried to stay as standard with the spellings as I could have. For instance, it is very common to use the word Mohammed in modern spellings, but Muhammad and Mohammad are equally common. When I was spelling the Prophet's name I tried to use the word Mohammed as universally as I could, but this was impossible to keep up throughout the entire work due to the fact that sometimes I would be quoting someone directly, or possibly the name was spelled a different way in one of the references if it was in the title of a book or article. Some examples other these disagreements:

"Khadija" for "Khadijah"
"Waraqa" for "Waraqah"
"Qu'ran" for "Quran" for "Koran"

Et cetera…

I have tried my best to not make this a heavy academic tome and to make it as readable as possible for all interested.

Also, there are some common themes that jump back and forth in Jack Chick's rendering of Alberto Rivera's testimony. This makes my refutations in several places seem like a rehash of what has already been said. I have tried to avoid this when possible but there were times that avoiding the repetition would have made it impossible to point out a misrepresentation in the Rivera story. I apologize for the situations where this has been unavoidable.

Finally, there are times in the book when I quoted people who have not been noted as a source. Each of these people have been interviewed personally by me either face-to-face, over the phone or over e-mail and are listed in the acknowledgements at the end of this book. These are all people who have the necessary backgrounds to qualify for commentary on the subject at hand. You will find that in the text of this book brief description of this person is given along with their quotations.

It is important to know that the first section of every chapter that is in *italics* is directly quoted from the story circulating the web "How the Vatican Created Islam", which is taken directly from the Chick Publication <u>The Prophet</u>. The rest of each chapter discusses this section of testimony. Also in the appendix section of this book you can find the full text of "How the Vatican Created Islam" which was taken directly from David Icke's website, which is in turn taken almost word-for-word from the tract.

If you have any questions or comments about what I have written, you are welcome to contact me at: g.d.cearley@gmail.com.

I hope you enjoy the book!

Gary Dale Cearley

Introduction

Freedom of religion is something that we in the United States have always prided ourselves on. For every religion or creed there is someone who finds hope, justice, inspiration, salvation, God…

I believe that we should always be mindful and respectful of others' beliefs. I demand that others are respectful of my own so I personally insure to give them the same. This is why this book exists.

Not long ago I was sent by e-mail the text to "How the Vatican Created Islam" by an acquaintance in Canada. This title was so incredible that it immediately caught my eye. Was there something I had missing in all my years of reading and studying and traveling? I printed it out to take home. As I was scanning over it with my eyes several of the statements in the testimony seemed just as out of place as the title did when I read it originally. But I sat it aside and didn't pay any attention. About a week later I was forwarded the David Icke Newsletter by another person, and lo and behold, in the newsletter was the story "How the Vatican Created Islam". This time the mail was coming from New Zealand. I took the writing a bit more seriously this go around. Then I got an e-mail with the same story again from someone in the United States. I had to take this piece of writing very seriously by this point and vowed myself to search out exactly what parts of this story were true and what parts of this story were total fabrications.

As I read the text much more carefully again at home I couldn't understand why someone would write this. I also couldn't understand why so many people were posting this up on websites. It was on hundreds of websites and blogs. The text was one that is almost completely lifted from a Jack Chick biblical tract in the form of a comic book, <u>The Prophet</u>, so I looked up the tract and read it cover to cover. And I studied its illustrations as well. I started at first spot checking to see if I could see immediately factual mistakes I could find without using a reference book. The mistakes were legion. Then I decided I would go deeper and started to look some of the incredible claims up in books that I have and as well as conducting a broad overview on the internet and through other sources, such as speaking with experts. I found literally hundreds of mistakes, not only historical mistakes, but mistakes in the basic logic of the story as well. I then began to see clearly something very sinister was before my eyes. These were not mistakes. I felt that this had the markings of an intentionally crafted story that only had the purpose of slandering Roman Catholicism and Islam, not a story written to impart any truth!

This slander was something that I felt when I was reading this text for the first time but did not want to fully see, mainly because I had always tried to keep an open mind when exploring new ideas that have been introduced to me during my time here on this earth. But the more I read *"How the Vatican Created Islam"* the more I began to see the fruits of pure hatred sewn into the text. I began to see a narrow mindedness that was so intent on its own purpose, on its own self importance and on its own singular definition of truth that it fostered a self perpetual disregard for honesty. I saw what I feel to be a quasi-religious bigot taking the guise of a Christian.

In my life I have not believed the same theology as either Roman Catholics or Muslims (or many other faiths for that matter). I was raised and brought up in the Churches of Christ. And yes, I will put it up front. We believe that we have the right way to live and that we will be going to Heaven. We pity souls who we reason won't get to Heaven because they don't believe like us and refuse to see the light. I suppose that everyone in my little home town of Prescott, Arkansas, where I went to school and church, felt the same or similar when they went to church and when they prayed. But we all have one thing in common. Everyday we find it in our hearts to love our brothers and our neighbors. We call it community. We call it Christian love. If we disagreed with the way some of our brothers, sisters and neighbors worshipped we spoke to them, made examples of our lives, or we simply ignored the behaviors or beliefs they harbored. We did not create vicious lies about how their faiths were born. And after having traveled around the world seeing many countries on several continents in both the northern and southern hemispheres I would dare say that most people alive in the world are similar to the people in my hometown of Prescott when it comes to living out your religion.

When I researched this story *"How the Vatican Created Islam"* and its source <u>The Prophet</u> by Jack Chick, I didn't see this Christian love that I was used to. I saw ignorance and paranoia. The point of the book, Alberto Rivera's testimony, was not to scare people into salvation, like many of Chick's earlier tracts. The purpose was to make you feel fear and hatred of both the Roman Catholics and Muslims. In this comic tract saw fabrications and outright lying to the point of being pathological. This lying only had the aim of falsely and harshly condemning followers of Roman Catholicism and Islam. And most shameful of all, I saw this from two men claiming to be men of God.

To get another view of the situation I turned the tables and tried to see this comic book tract, <u>The Prophet</u>, as a Catholic or a Muslim would read it, and again I felt shame. Not for my own religious beliefs, but for what these two supposed men of God, Jack Chick, who wrote and published the book, and Alberto Rivera, who provided the testimony for this book, were doing to us all. To the Protestants, Chick and Rivera make the Catholics and Muslims look evil. And to the Catholics and Muslims, Chick and Rivera make the Protestants look evil for coming up with such slanderous untruths. The only thing this type book does is to foster mutual fear, mutual disrespect and mutual hatred. I don't call that Christian.

I think it is important to add here that when I first read this testimony it took a bit of time for this all to sink in. I may have been bad at times in my life, and I don't claim and have never claimed to be the best person around. But I am not looking for evil in everything, so it took me a little longer to see this facet of Jack Chick's rendition of Alberto Rivera's "testimony". Yet, as I dug deeper I began to feel this hatred of the "other" bearing down on me.

A funny thing that came out of all this research, which I consider a testimony to the kind of Christians attracted to Jack Chick's mantras, was that when I contacted some of the writers who had been published by Jack Chick's company, Chick Publications, to see whether they would be able to help me with this text from a doctrinal standpoint. (Was there something I was missing in the text?) Two of those I contacted were Rick Jones and Dr. Robert Morey. Neither bothered to even respond. Personally I would have thought Dr. Morey would have been hot to respond, as he is one of the leading critics of the Islamic religion today, but I guess I was wrong.

Another expert who I tried to contact for background help on my project, Dr. Ergun Mehmet Caner, deleted my e-mail without even reading it. I considered Dr. Caner to be indirectly related to Chick Publication's positions on Islam because Dr. Caner's book, Unveiling Islam (which was co-written with his brother Dr. Emir Fethi Caner and published by Kregel Publications), is on sale on the Chick Publications website. Chick Publications also provides author bios of Ergun and Emir Caner. I considered this promotion to be a likely mutual endorsement of one another's points of view. Dr. Caner would have been an excellent person to have helping me on this book. Why? Many reasons:

1) He was born a Muslim (he is Turkish) and converted against his family's wishes to Christianity;

2) He has written or co-written four books directly or indirectly about Islam;

3) He is high profile in the American national media, having been on national television and in numerous print publications on several occasions;

4) He is the dean of the Jerry Falwell founded Liberty University's Liberty Theological Seminary of Lynchburg, Virginia; and

5) One of the courses Dr. Caner teaches at Liberty Theological Seminary is Church History.

I have to express some disappointment that Dr. Ergun Caner never responded to my request as I feel that he would have been a man who would have liked to have seen the truth come out of this story. Maybe in the future Dr. Caner will not let such opportunities pass so easily.

On a more personal note I must say quite frankly, part of me did not feel good about pushing forward with this personal project of mine. I remembered with an almost fondness the tracts from Chick Publications even from the first church of my memory, the Hickory Grove Church of Christ. It was a little church in the Hickory Grove countryside community up the road from where I spent my earliest years of memory, on Nevada County Rural Route 3. I can remember snagging these tracts at church when no one was looking and taking them home with me. These tracts weren't for children necessarily.

They were for witnessing Jesus to the world. But the artwork drew my attention and kept it. The tracts were very basic, but easy to read and easy to understand. I always got the message: *Give your life to Jesus now or face eternal damnation!* When the Hickory Grove Church of Christ was forced to close (we had no full-time preacher and the congregation was mainly older folks – younger families often attended church in town, and our attendance averages were in the twenties) my whole family moved to the Prescott Church of Christ. In those days Jack Chick's tracts were a familiar sight at that congregation as well, and might even still be today. I always thought "this cartoonist must really be a man of God..."

I guess it would be easy to believe in thinking back then that Jack Chick must really love the Lord. As long as you aren't a Jew... Or a Mormon... Or a Muslim... Or a Catholic...

In re-reading Jack Chick today I really had to set myself aside and look at the tract as a whole, and impartially, which wasn't easy to do. But I came to the conclusion that a person's salvation is nothing if it isn't based in honesty. God won't accept a prayer when it doesn't come from your heart. Why should we fool ourselves to believe that it is okay to lie to people and about other people if we are only trying to save the people we are lying to? The people you are trying to help will only resent you for your hypocrisy when they discover it. I concluded that you won't save anyone like that. But you may lose yourself. You can't preach that God is love and then show hatred.

Nevertheless I pushed through the research and contacted some ministers and professors through friends, networks I belong to, directories and websites that these people kept as well as lay several lay people with specialized interests on the subjects of Early Christian History, Early Islamic History, etc. In many cases the people felt they might not be expert enough to help out or they were just too busy. This is understandable. I also contacted experts on Judaism, Catholicism and Islam from whatever religious affiliation they may have been. By and by several people also helped and made this project possible.

But I really noticed one thing about the religious family I was supposed to belong to, the Southern Protestants who grew out of the Second Great Awakening movement of the nineteenth century, the Fundamental Baptists, the Churches of Christ, the Pentecostals... And though it may not seem fair to say, it was something that disturbed me. I am not talking about simply the non-replies of the Chick Publications authors and the deleted e-mail from Dr. Ergun Caner. Few, very few of the evangelicals trusted me and what I was trying to do by writing this book. Very few trusted me at all.

A few short examples: One Texas based person who had a tract ministry on the web would refuse to give me his name. He would purport to be studying me. He looked up my website. He quoted me back my political affiliation. He asked me my beliefs, but he held his cards very close to his chest and would not help me with any information. What on earth was he trying to hide? Did he think he was protecting someone?

Another prime example I found was Steve Van Nattan, a supposed religious man who was in Tennessee. Van Nattan is an evangelical who has researched Islam and put his findings on his website. I also knew that this man had already done some substantial research on some of the problems of the claims of Jack Chick's tracts concerning Roman Catholicism. But Steve Van Nattan refused to discuss any of this with me at all, period. Without even asking my personal beliefs (other than a one liner asking "who was Jesus to me?") and only caring what church I belonged to he out of hand called me a "heretic" who was doomed to Hell and told me to just "drop it". Van Nattan added that he would not be helping someone who was going to Hell, even if it was helping to refute "Catholics". I told him that I wasn't interested in discussing doctrine with him, only the facts of the testimony. He again called me a heretic and told me I was doomed to Hell. End of story as far as he was concerned.

Maybe it was the wrong thing to do, but in response to being called twice a heretic, in response I called him something that will stay here on this earth.

As I mentioned before, but I want to drive the point home, in this book I am not going to attack Jack Chick or Alberto Rivera or anyone else on what they believe to be the truth about their own religion, about their own road to Heaven or Hell. I do think these folks, Jack

Chick, Alberto Rivera, and Steve Van Nattan in Tennessee for that matter, make themselves into sad, little people for doing so themselves. It is very unfortunate that anyone has to be that way. But what I will say is that I will hit bone crunching hard at the facts of their testimony about others. Jack Chick's and Alberto Rivera's testimony won't survive the trial by fire that the truth brings with it. Alberto Rivera has been dead for many years and Jack Chick is already in his eighties. I don't expect to change them with this book. It is a bit too late I would reckon. But this book will be there as a monument to the folly they have created and as an answer to any person who wants to know what kind of testimony they give. This book will be there to show that they were not the Christians the purported to be. I personally believe that you cannot even truly believe in God at all if you don't have a regard for the truth because God is the very nature of truth.

I always was taught that the word "Christian" was both a noun and an adjective meaning "Christ like". Chick and Rivera aren't making us more like Jesus Christ by creating these untruthful slanders against the Roman Catholics and Muslims, or even the Jews, the Jehovah's Witnesses, the Latter Day Saints, and any of the others rolled over by these fake histories. I have never, ever heard of Jesus creating false histories of those who disagreed with him. As such, I offer this book to anyone else who feels the same as I do and wishes to not stand for it anymore.

I already know the effect of this book will be powerful. I know because the last time I looked at the twentieth chapter of Exodus "Thou shalt not bear false witness" was still a commandment. One of the commandments that show us how we all should live.

Traction

Jack Thomas Chick was born April 13, 1924, in the Boyle Heights part of Los Angeles. The year1924 as it turns out was a leap year, and historically it was quite eventful....

This was the year that Vladimir Lenin died. And Stalin came to power. Mohandas Gandhi is released from prison. GMT is first broadcasted hourly from the Royal Greenwich Observatory. Nevada becomes the first US state to use a gas chamber for executions. Gershwin's "Rhapsody in Blue" is first performed. International Business Machines (IBM) is founded. Calvin Coolidge becomes the first president to deliver a radio broadcast from the White House. The Ottoman Empire collapses when Kemal Atatürk's Young Turks rise to power. Adolf Hitler goes to jail for his Beer Hall Putsch. Greece becomes a republic. J. Edgar Hoover becomes the head of the Federal Bureau of Investigation. Nathan Leopold, Jr. and Richard Loeb murdered 14-year-old Bobby Franks in cold blood in Chicago just to see if they could get away with it. Native Americans finally get the rights of United States citizenship. Nellie Tayloe Ross of Wyoming elected as the first woman governor in the United States. The first Macy's Thanksgiving Day Parade is held in New York City. The highest grossing film in 1924 was "The Thief of Baghdad", starring Douglas Fairbanks.

As you can see the world was very busy the year Jack Chick was born.

Jack's mother, Pauline, who was only twenty when Jack was born, reportedly tried to abort him but was unsuccessful.[1] While he was still young Jack's family moved curiously enough to nearby Alhambra, southeast of Los Angeles. This is an odd footnote because Alhambra is the named of the Moorish castle in Spain that was built by the Nasrid Muslim rulers. It was an Islamic political center until the Christians ran the Muslims out of the area in 1492. Jack Chick would have loved them.

Jack wasn't the healthiest kid around, but he made do. It is said that the Chick family doctor had to lance his ears over 20 times before he was a year old. Maybe this had something to do with his creative side. Jack was very artistic from his early childhood, and was keen about doodling and drawing. Chick claimed that this pre-occupation of drawing caused him to be held back in first grade because he was so busy drawing airplanes in battle to keep up with his work. The older Jack got the more he continued to draw. It was in high school that Jack gained an active interest in theater arts and became a member of the school's drama club. He gained a two year scholarship to the Pasadena Playhouse School of Theater, which had been opened since 1928 and in 1937 designated as California's official state theater, after he finished his high school diploma in 1942, but World War II interrupted his studies there.

---

[1] According to Robert Ito in his article "To Hell with You", The Independent on Sunday, July 6th, 2003

After Chick's stints in Australia, Papua New Guinea and later Japan, with the United States Army Jack returned to the Pasadena Playhouse. The Playhouse was thriving despite having gone through the long war years. Part of this stemmed from the fact that immediately after the Second World War the GI bill boosted the student population even more than before. During this time there were several famous actors who studied there, such as Raymond Burr, Eve Arden and Charles Bronson. In years to follow the likes of Dustin Hoffman and Gene Hackman would also become noted alumni. And it was during Chick's second tenure at the Playhouse that he met his bride to be, the 21 year old Lola Lynn, who he married in 1948.

Jack and Lola spent their honeymoon time in Canada to visit her family. But Lola Lynn's family were born again Christians and were not impressed with Jack's un-Christian ways. During this time, Jack Chick had not yet become active in the Christian faith. He had not found God.

By his own admission, Jack had a foul-mouth which dated from his teenaged years. This habit of using bad language most likely was intensified during the time of his military service as well as after, when Jack was around "theater types". Lola's family on the other hand was more pious and followed a very fundamentalist, evangelical lifestyle. While on his visit with them, Jack was forced to listen to Charles E. Fuller's Old-Fashioned Revival Hour radio show, which oddly enough, was coincidentally based in the Los Angeles area where Jack Chick was from.[2]   Through this radio show and Lola's mother's influence Jack was saved. Jack's conversion was complete to the point that he spent years dreaming of becoming a missionary.[3] Charles E. Fuller became a lasting influence on Jack Chick.

Chick today is an Independent Fundamentalist Baptist, known as Congregationalists. They hold Baptist beliefs but not Baptist formal organization. He is a "King James Only" leader who is part of a movement that doesn't believe modern translations of the Bible can be trusted. He is also a pre-millennial dispensationalist who believes that a terrible tribulation will descend on the earth and its inhabitants for seven years before the second coming of Christ, but that true Christian believers will be lifted out of this world and saved. These saved Christians will not have the horrible experiences prophesied of the "last days".[4]

---

[2] This radio show by Dr. Charles E. Fuller was a pioneer in religious programming. It broadcasted from a studio in Hollywood in the year 1925, moving to the Long Beach Municipal Auditorium by 1941 where it stayed until 1958, when it moved back to a studio for a 30 minute recorded session. It first broadcast to a wide audience of 13 stations on the Mutual Network in 1937. During World War II thousands of servicemen attended the broadcast services and would travel around the United States holding citywide services. By 1951 the broadcast circled the globe via 650 stations on the ABC radio network and remained on the air until the death of Charles Fuller in December of 1968. The Old Fashioned Revival Hour radio show is still available on scores of stations around the United States, short wave radio and on internet radio.

[3] Lola was against Jack becoming a missionary and based on her perception of the dangers missionaries encountered. This was based upon a family experience when her aunt was a missionary in Africa. At the time Lola's aunt was pregnant and being carried across a river on a stretcher. One of the men helping to carry the pregnant lady lost a leg to a crocodile. Chick's website says it was an "alligator" but alligators only live in the United States and China so it had to be a crocodile.

[4] As described in Matthew 24:37-41.

Jack Chick was not only influenced by Charles E. Fuller, but also by other Christian radio broadcasts. But one in particular helped give rise to Jack's idea of publication of religious comic tracts. In Chicago the Pacific Garden Mission, a well established entity which dates from 1877, began producing a Christian radio drama called "UNSHACKLED!". This program was first aired on the radio station WGN in 1950.

UNSHACKLED!'s first episode was about the baseball player turned evangelist, Billy Sunday. These shows were personal accounts of people giving their souls to Christ and changing their lives. The next step for the producers of these shows was to begin production of these stories as small comic books. Most of these small illustrated books were based on some of the more popular shows that had aired which could be effectively used as religious tracts. Although Jack Chick later purported that he got the idea for his religious cartoon tracts after being told by Bob Hammond[5] that Chinese communist propaganda was often successfully spread to the peasants via cartoon tracts, the UNSHACKLED! tracts obviously had a huge influence on his work.

Jack Chick had always wanted to be an illustrator since his early years, but until he had actually gone into the business himself, he had to satisfy himself with working as a technical illustrator at the Astro Science Corporation in El Monte, next door to his childhood home of

---

[5] Robert Bruce Hammond, 1914 - 2002, grew up in both Hong Kong and San Pedro, California. He was a missionary to Southeast Asia and was interred in a Japanese prison camp in Hong Kong in 1941. He had a radio ministry in the United States called "Voice of China and Asia" for nearly five decades.

Alhambra. It was during this time that Jack started the hobby of illustrating tracts. Jack was sitting in his car reading a copy of Charles Grandison Finney's "Power From On High"[6] given him by an old welder. After going to church Chick noticed what he described as "all the deadness and hypocrisy" and wondered why there was no revival, such as Finney had promoted. Chick then started the religious drawings in order to wake up Christians in their beliefs in order to pray for revival. His first tract would carry the title "Why No Revival?". Jack had a problem in though in that he couldn't find a publisher. As such Chick was forced to self-publish and borrowed $800 from a credit union to get started. Chick founded his own company (originally based in his kitchen) soon afterward. A short time later "A Demon's Nightmare", Chick's first evangelical tract was written. Jack claimed he wrote the text for this in 15 minutes and the owner of Astro Science, Jack's boss, paid for the first printing.

Today Jack Chick is well known for his button pushing comic-style tracts comic books that are pure hell-fire and brimstone content. These publications are pure and heavy evangelism and all are from a Hell fire God fearing fundamentalist perspective. The pocket-sized tracts are graphic, quite often dealing with the leading characters'

---

[6] Many of the chapters in this book, "Power From On High" were originally published in "The Independent" in New York, and date from 1871-74. The book was first compiled and published in 1944, nearly seven decades after the author's death. Charles Grandison Finney (1792–1875), originally a Presbyterian, was a well known Congregationalist minister often referred to as "America's foremost revivalist". Although Finney never attended college himself, he later became president of Oberlin College in Ohio. Finney was a leader of the "Second Great Awakening" which led to many converts in the Baptist and Methodist congregations and gave rise to the Disciples of Christ and Churches of Christ.

deaths in order to bring home either their eternal salvation or eternal damnation. On the way through you will see murders, violence, devils… Chick wants to scare you into salvation.

But Jack Chick, according to some, has gone out of his way with the truth.

In many of the tracts Chick turns his sites to what he and others who share his beliefs call "false religions". His biggest, most preposterous claims have been aimed at two groups in particular: The Roman Catholic Church and Islam. Going a few steps beyond what even conspiracy theorists would dare say, Jack Chick has claimed that the Catholic Church is descendant from the ancient pagan religion of Babylon and that the pope is an agent of Satan and has commanded the Nazi army during the Second World War. He has blamed the United States civil war, the Lincoln assassination and the founding of the Ku Klux Klan on "Catholic infiltrators", particularly Jesuits.

George Kozak, the parish deacon of the Immaculate Conception in Ithaca, New York, has heard it all before. "Jack Chick usually uses a 'former Jesuit' to tell his tales of intrigue, so I am not surprised that this story starts with 'a former Jesuit'," said Kozak, "Of course, it is all nonsense. Anyone familiar with Islam and early Church history can tell it is nonsense."

Unfortunately not everyone has the grounding in early Christian History or early Islamic History and this is what the Chick Publication tract is playing on. George Kozak is not as easy as others to swallow the hook, but then again, he's a bit more than a lay person or an innocent bystander who got caught off guard with the false claims. George has been ordained as a deacon since 1998 and hold's a Master of Theology from Saint Bernard's Institute in Rochester, New York. George finds that these kinds of fundamentalist early Christian History revisionisms tend to follow a common pattern.

"People like Jack Chick always claim the Catholic Church was a creation of Constantine and the 'real' Christians were subjugated by these 'fake' Christians. Any reading of history will show you how false that claim is," said Kozak, "Occasionally, he [Jack Chick] intersperses his false history with true facts like 'Mohammed's father died when he was young' or the 'Temple was destroyed in 70 AD', but most of it is so off-base. In my opinion, this is the same sort of 'history' that Dan Brown uses in the "Da Vinci Code" to prove that Jesus was married to Mary Magdalene and she is the Holy Grail. This is a 'history' that is not based on fact."

Kurt Kuersteiner, the author of The Unofficial Guide to the Art of Jack T. Chick: Chick Tracts, Crusader Comics, And Battle Cry Newspapers, is a bit tempered about where Jack Chick is coming from. "Yes, Chick is a fundamentalist, and that orthodox branch [of Christian fundamentalism] has been critical of Catholics for a long time," remarked Kuersteiner, "One of the reasons is because they were systematically persecuted and executed by Catholics back in the days of the Inquisition. Whether you agree with Chick's beliefs is really based on whether you are a literalist or not. If you are, he has some compelling arguments that are difficult to dismiss. If you are not, it is easy to wave off his claims as being politically incorrect."

Chick's claims regarding Catholicism's role in the birth Islam are the subject matter of the rest of this book. This claim centers around one source: Alberto Magno Romero Rivera

To say the very least, Alberto Rivera is an extremely controversial figure. "I consider his testimony to be a lot like those of people who have seen UFOs," said Kuersteiner, "They MAY be telling the truth, but it is outside our experience, so it's difficult to believe since we've never seen a UFO ourselves. Yet it is impossible to prove they are mistaken. So I guess I'm saying you really have to decide on these matters yourself. The uncertainty of it is one of the aspects that makes Chick so fascinating."

Alberto Rivera is the narrator and protagonist of many of Jack Chick's comic books and tracts. Rivera is the main character in no less than six issues of Chick's "The Crusaders" full-size comic books which began printing in the 1970's.

Rivera is also the source of much of Jack Chick's most questionable testimony.

But who was Alberto Rivera? What do we know about this man? Was he for real? Did he mean well? Or was he a charlatan?

Alberto Magno Romero Rivera, a Spaniard, was born in 1937 in the Canary Islands. He claimed to have been a Jesuit priest who had served many times as an undercover operative of with orders from the Jesuits to infiltrate and destroy Protestant churches and institutions in Spain and also in Venezuela and Costa Rica. He claimed he was later rewarded by being secretly ordained as a bishop. Yet through many questionable instances in his life and through earnest, secret study of the Bible, and through reflection on God's nature, Rivera secretly became a born again Christian. For this change of heart, Rivera maintained that the Catholic Church kept him a physical prisoner, interrogated him in a quasi-prison like sanatorium run by the Catholic Church, and then expelled him with a ticket out of Spain with and only forty cents in his pocket.

In the 1970s he met Jack Chick, who ate Rivera's story up and regurgitated it upon society. It refined Chick's beliefs about the Catholic Church which smacked of global conspiracy paranoia. Rivera, together with another Jack Chick source, John Todd,[7] laid claim that the Pope, Jesuits and other Catholic institutions not only founded Islam, but were behind the US Civil War, assassination of Abraham Lincoln, created Jehovah's Witnesses, controls the mafia, started Communism, was behind the Holocaust (or at least complicit),

---

[7] John Wayne Todd, who was also known as "John Todd Collins", "Lance Collins", and "Christopher Kollyns" is an evangelical minister who claimed to have been born into a 'witchcraft family' before converting to Christianity. He has authored several books, mainly about the occult, which are printed by Chick Publications.

created the Church of Jesus Christ of Latter Day Saints, and on and on...

Of course Muslims and Roman Catholics are expected to be upset over Chick and Rivera's outrageous claims, which are often more outlandish than the Da Vinci Code's "revelations" but there have been many Protestants and Evangelicals who took deep offense at the allegations Rivera made. Alberto Rivera's comments through Jack Chick's religious publications were becoming the "face of the evangelicals" to many outsiders. It was unfair and it was wrong. Because of this several people who were strong in the evangelical churches felt it their duty to look into the life that Alberto Rivera lived and where he got his outrageous claims.

It did not take a microscope to see the bacteria.

Alberto Rivera's accusations are covered in many books and publications. Notable among the refutations are Karl Keating's <u>The Usual Suspects: Answering Anti-Catholic Fundamentalists</u>.[8] Several Christian publications[9] have also printed articles exposing Alberto Rivera as not only a religious fraud, but even a crook sought after by

[8] Ignatius Press, 2000
[9] "Alberto Rivera: Is He For Real?", Christianity Today, March 13, 1981
"The Alberto Story," Gary Metz. Cornerstone Magazine, vol. 9, no. 53, 1981, pp. 29-31
"The Force and Alberto Rivera", The Quarterly Journal, Vol 3, No 4.
"Alberto: The Truth About His Story", Brian Onken, Christian Research Journal, 981 Volume: 4 Number: 2
"Religious Hoax of the Century: The True Story of Alberto Rivera Uncovered", Leslie Price, Evangelicals Now Magazine, November 2000

the authorities, claiming that Rivera had warrants in Florida for a stolen a credit card and money run up on its account as well as a warrant for taking an unauthorized vehicle which he apparently abandoned in Seattle. There were also accusations that Rivera collected money for a Spanish charity (a learning institution) that was apparently not paid in to the intended charity, written checks on closed accounts, was sued for swindling over $2000 related to church property.

Over the course of time several noted Protestant publications, including Christianity Today, Cornerstone, etc., conducted checks and investigations which unanimously uncovered Alberto Rivera as a fraud. But even looking into the face of the evidence concerning Alberto Rivera's fraudulent lifestyle, Chick and several others continued to defend and support Alberto Rivera.

Alberto Rivera has since passed away. Officially it was colon cancer. Jack Chick believes that the Jesuits finally got him with a secret poison that was designed in order to give Rivera his slow, painful death. They had been trying to assassinate poor Brother Alberto for decades, ever since Rivera since he left the Roman Catholic Church. According to a Catholic journalist, Jimmy Akin…

> "Alberto was murdered, you know," Jack informed
> me.
>
> "Well, I understand that he had cancer, but beyond that
> I'm not aware of anything," I replied.

"Oh, yes, he was murdered." Jack went on to say that he had been told by an ex-member of the IRA of two poisons, one of which causes cancer. "And that was what they gave him."[10]

Why should we care what information Chick and Rivera put out? Jack Chick and Alberto Rivera had every right to believe what they want and to say what they wanted.

Jack Chick and Alberto Rivera have committed in my opinion nothing more than religious slander. They presented falsehoods that they purported to be facts and disseminated these to worldwide audiences. Jack Chick is continuing to disseminate these books, tracts and comics under the name of God.

When I say "falsehoods", I am not speaking now about religious dogmas. It is not for me to say how they can believe about their salvation and interpret the Bible. I am speaking about slandering someone else's beliefs by creating false historical settings. I am speaking about their creations of scenarios and historical settings which distort history in an attempt to blacken the leaders and followers of their religious targets.

I have some indexes in the back of the book that deal with Alberto Rivera's personal life and Jack Chick's stubborn ignoring of the facts. I leave that to the people who have already done these hard yards.

---

[10] "Meet Jack Chick: A Conversation with the Granddaddy of the Anti-Catholic Comic Book Genre", by Jimmy Akin, This Rock Magazine, Volume 15, Number 3, March, 2004

The rest of this book is devoted to one tract that Jack Chick publishes. It comes in the form of a comic book that is narrated by Alberto Rivera. This publication is called <u>The Prophet</u> and is the sixth book of Chick Publications. In my critique of this narrative I will not touch on Chick's or Rivera's relationship with God or what they believed to be the means of salvation. I will stick strictly to what Rivera's testimony is and what the actual true story is. I will only look at the well documented historical facts and directly compare them to Alberto Rivera's story. It should be an interesting read if you, like me, find history fascinating.

Let's begin…

The Vatican's Secret Problem

"What I'm going to tell you is what I learned in secret briefings in the Vatican when I was a Jesuit priest, under oath and induction. A Jesuit cardinal named Augustine Bea showed us how desperately the Roman Catholics wanted Jerusalem at the end of the third century. Because of its religious history and its strategic location, the Holy City was considered a priceless treasure. A scheme had to be developed to make Jerusalem a Roman Catholic city.

"The great untapped source of manpower that could do this job was the children of Ishmael. The poor Arabs fell victim to one of the most clever plans ever devised by the powers of darkness. Early Christians went everywhere with the gospel setting up small churches, but they met heavy opposition. Both the Jews and the Roman government persecuted the believers in Christ to stop their spread. But the Jews rebelled against Rome, and in 70 AD, Roman armies under General Titus smashed Jerusalem and destroyed the great Jewish temple which was the heart of Jewish worship...in fulfillment of Christ's prophecy in Matthew 24:2.

"On this holy placed today where the temple once stood, the Dome of the Rock Mosque stands as Islam's second most holy place. Sweeping changes were in the wind. Corruption, apathy, greed, cruelty, perversion and rebellion were eating at the Roman Empire, and it was ready to collapse. The persecution against Christians was useless as they continued to lay down their lives for the gospel of Christ.

The Prophet, by Jack T. Chick, Chick Publications, 1988

To start off with, just who was this Jesuit Cardinal "Augustine Bea" who Alberto Rivera claims all of this story came from?

None of the Alberto Rivera "testimonies" say for sure. The most likely would have been a man named "Augustin" (note the spelling difference). Augustin Cardinal Bea SJ was a cardinal in the Roman Catholic Church whose most noteworthy achievement being that he was appointed as the first President of the Vatican's Secretariat for Promoting Christian Unity, now called the Pontifical Council for Promoting Christian Unity. This council was founded by Pope John XXIII on June 5th, 1960. The purpose for this organization is to promote official dialogue between the Roman Catholic Church, the Eastern Orthodox and Ancient Oriental Churches as well as several Western denominations, such as the Lutheran, Anglican and Baptist Churches.

Since June 28th, 1988 the council has been a permanent dicastry (department) of the Holy See, seated in the Vatican. From 1964 onward Cardinal Bea's assistant was the highly controversial Irish priest Father Malachi Martin who wrote several books damning the Roman Catholic Church. Alberto Rivera is never mentioned in these books, nor does he ever mention these books in any Chick publication. Taking into regard the fact that Alberto Rivera claimed to have served covertly in Spain, Venezuela and Costa Rica before returning to Spain and being forcedly interned in a Spanish Catholic sanatorium,[11] coupled with the fact that his very service in the priesthood was even doubtful, it is highly improbable that he would have even met Augustin Cardinal Bea.

Putting the doubtful acquaintance with Cardinal Bea aside, the first and most glaring outright falsehood in the above is that the Roman Catholic Church could even think in terms of political strategy in the third century. The early Christians in Rome, and indeed throughout the entire Roman Empire, suffered from very intense persecution until finally Christianity was legalized by the Edict of Milan in the fourth century (313 AD). Constantine I jointly issued the Edict of Milan with Licinius, the Eastern Roman Emperor and only from 380 AD onwards was Christianity the officially favored religion by the Roman Empire.

Ralph Williams, a former missionary in the Ukraine who studied Early Christian History at Harding University and later went to graduate school at the University of Memphis, would even go so far as to say that the Roman Catholic Church was still very embryonic, and was not even known by that name or form during that time period concerned in The Prophet. "The 'Roman Catholic Church' didn't exist in the third century, when this fellow [Alberto Rivera] claims that this conspiracy was born," said Williams "During the first three centuries, the church suffered persecution, often official persecution, but more often, persecution that was not sanctioned by the government. It wasn't until the fourth century that Constantine

---

[11] Alberto, Chick Publications, 1979

converted to Christianity, and his empire was centered in Constantinople,[12] not in Rome. Constantine didn't make Christianity the official religion of the Roman empire; that didn't happen until the end of the 4th century, under Theodosius I."[13]

George Kozak is in agreement. "The Roman Church was not all that powerful at that time [during the third century]," explains deacon Kozak, "In fact, the power-base of the Church were the Eastern Churches. Most of the early Councils and theology was developed in the East. The early Church was concerned with survival, Barbarian invasions and working out their theologies... The Church wasn't desperate for capturing Jerusalem at the end of the third century. It was part of the Roman Empire. Any Christian could travel there and there were Churches there."

In the fourth century things were changed drastically for the Christians. As mentioned earlier, Christianity was legalized and even treated as the *de facto* state religion, the various churches throughout the Roman and Constantinople controlled areas quickly grew and prospered. The First Council of Nicaea in 325 AD gave Christian,

---

[12] In 320 AD, Licinius, emperor of the Eastern Roman Empire, began ignoring the religious freedom secured by the Edict of Milan in 313 AD Licinius began another persecution of the Christians. This was a direct challenge to Constantine and the Christians because the edict had been issued in both the names so Constantine and Licinius. Constantine raised a Christian army to fight against Licinius's pagan army and eventually won full control of the Eastern Roman Empire, renaming Byzantium as Nova Roma and establishing a senate there.

[13] Flavius Theodosius (347 – 395 AD), also known as "Theodosius the Great".

Eastern Roman and Oriental, the Nicene Creed[14] in an attempt to unify the beliefs of Christians everywhere. And until being made the official state religion at the end of the fourth century there was only one major lull… The reign of Julian the Apostate.

"The last pagan Roman Emperor was Julian the Apostate,[15] who tried to re-establish Roman traditional religions as well as other religious traditions within the Empire on an equal footing with Christianity," said Len Rosen, who studied Islamic Studies and Medieval History at the University of Toronto, "He failed because Christianity had become so predominant in all its various forms within the Empire by the middle 300s that putting it on equal footing was counter-intuitive."

More on that later…

---

[14] The Nicene Creed was adopted at the First Council of Nicaea in 325 AD. The purpose of the Nicene Creed was to establish conformity of belief for all Christians which would be considered uniquely essential for Christians. By profession of the creed each community would be able to recognize heresies and deviations within their churches. Constantine I invited all of the bishops of Christendom, about 1000 in the East and 800 in the West of the Roman Empire, but only about an estimated 300 actually made the journey. Of this number the vast majority were eastern bishops whereas only five were from the Western Roman Empire. This number did not include the Bishop of Rome, Pope Sylvester I, as he was ill. Instead he sent two priests as observer representatives. See: And Would You Believe It?: The Story of the Nicene Creed, Bernard Basset, Sheed and Ward, 1976

[15] Flavius Claudius Iulianus (331 – 363), was the last Pagan Roman Emperor who ruled in the middle of the fourth century. Julian was born a Greek in Constantinople, originally pagan but raised Christian by a zealous relative, in later years he rebelled against Christianity, claiming it was "forced on him". He tried to restore the traditional worship as a measure to stop the decay of his world. Christians dubbed him "Julian the Apostate", because of his rejection of Christianity and conversion to a paganistic tradition known as "Theurgy". See: Julian's Gods: Religion and Philosophy in the Thought and Action of Julian the Apostate, Rowland Smith, Routledge, 1995

None of the Popes during the time period that Alberto Rivera demarcated were preoccupied with Jerusalem. Just to give a run down of accomplishments of the three Bishops of Rome were doing during the specific time period that Alberto Rivera noted (the end of the third century), I am giving a very brief synopsis of the popes (who they were and what they were known for) from 275 AD until 299 AD, the end of the third century.[16]

St. Eutychian (275 – 283 AD)

St. Eutychian succeeded Pope Felix I a few days after Felix I's death. We know no details of his pontificate except that he held his position as leader of the Church from January, 275 AD, until 7 December, 283 AD.

St. Gaius (283 – 296 AD)

Saint Gaius, also called Caius, was pope from 283 AD until his death in 296 AD. He related by family to the emperor Diocletian, and became pope on December 17, 283 AD.

St. Marcellinus (296 – 304 AD)

Saint Marcellinus ascended the papacy in the end of June 296 AD. He is not mentioned in the in the Depositio Episcoporum, the Martyrologium Hieronymianum, nor in the Depositio Martyrus. At the end of his reign Caesar Galerius began a movement to suppress Christianity, the Church's property was confiscated and religious

---

[16] The Catholic Encyclopedia, Volume XI, 1911 by Robert Appleton Company

writings were all destroyed. The Emperor, after fires in his home, ordered that Christians give up Christianity or face death.

Marcellinus was forced by Diocletian to offer incense to pagan gods and to defect his religion. Afterward Marcellinus repented, confessed his faith and suffered martyrdom. At the time of Marcellinus's death Armenia was the only Christian nation in the world, and they had only become so three years prior.

So even if Jerusalem had not been under Roman rule at the time, anyone would be able to see that none of these popes had their sights set on ruling Jerusalem. They were in no position to harbor such thoughts or plans.

Ralph Williams agrees. "All this conspiracy stuff sounds exciting, but it hardly fits with the facts," said Williams, "Christians in the third century were far more concerned with surviving and with defeating heresies like Gnosticism and Arianism that they encountered daily. Besides that, if you read the things they were writing, possession of Jerusalem, or any other city, was far from their minds. Even the heretics would have been horrified at the suggestion. Christianity was a spiritual religion, and didn't consider such physical things to be important. The Gnostic heresy illustrates this amply: the essence of Gnosticism was the denial of the physical in favor of the spiritual. They denied the physicality of the Christ; they would certainly have been horrified at the suggestion that Christianity ought to possess his physical birthplace. While arguing against Gnosticism and for the physicality and humanity of Christ, the church fathers would still not have started a conspiracy to take possession of Jerusalem, nor to drive the Jews, and 'false Christians' out of Jerusalem. It just doesn't fit in their thinking."

Again, during this time the Eastern Christian Churches were stronger in many ways compared with that of Rome and would continue to be so until the schism. "Even though the Roman Catholic Church claims that the papacy and the authority of the Papacy was handed down from Peter in Rome, that is a claim that was not made until very late in history," said Ralph Williams, "It's possible that some of the apostles lived until the early years of the second century; the people who knew the apostles lived almost until the third century. These are the people we know as the 'Church Fathers'. There was a great deal of controversy among them. Several of them spent their lives fighting against things they believed were contrary to Christian doctrine. There was a push to develop some consistent way of saying what true Christian doctrine was, and what was heresy, and so there was also a push toward some form of universal authority." But this universal authority didn't come until the Nicene Creed.

Rivera's claim about the Arabs being considered the children of Ishmael is basically true whether you look at it from a Judeo-Christian perspective or an Arab perspective. Arabs do regard themselves as the children of Ishmael. Indeed Mohammed himself claimed to be directly related to Adam via Ishmael.[17] But during the time period

---

[17] Muhammad a descendant of Ishmael: The oldest extant biography of Mohammad, which was compiled by Mohammed Ibn Ishak, and edited by Abu

that Alberto Rivera is referring to most of the Arabs were simple
Bedouins or were settled in the Hejaz or in Felix Arabia. Even the
Bedouins who moved around were fairly confined to the Arabian
Peninsula and parts of the region making up the modern day Kuwait,
southern regions of Iraq and the western Syriac regions. These
Bedouins are least likely to have been the people to take up a religious
mantle[18] against Christians, as per the reported conspiracy. So
regarding the assertion the Arabs were a "great untapped source of
manpower to use against the Christians", this is easily refuted.

Len Rosen weighs in again. "This is a simplification of Arab
history," says Rosen, "During the third century through the sixth
century there were a number of Arab client states that bordered both
the Roman and Persian empires. In the third century one of these
client kingdoms wrested Syria from the Roman Empire for more than
a decade, establishing a Kingdom with its centre in Palmyra.[19] In the
period before the rise of Mohammad, there were three significant

---

Mohammed Abd Al Malik Ibn Hisham, begins: "This book contains the life of the
Apostle of God: Muhammad was the son of Abd Allah, son of Abdu-l-Mottaleb,
son of Hashim, son of Abd Menaf, son of Kussei, son of Kilab, son of Murra, son of
Kaab, son of Luei, son of Ghalib, son of Fihr, son of Malik, son of Nadhr, son of
Kinana, son of Khuzeima, son of Mudrika, son of Alya, son of Mudhar, son of
Nizar, son of Maad, son of Adrian, son of Udd, son of Mukawwam, son of Nahor,
son of Teira, son of Yarob, son of Yashyob, son of Nabit, son of Ishmael, son of
Abraham, the Friend of God, son of Tara, son of Nahor, son of Sarukh, son of Rau,
son of Falih, son of Eiber, son of Shalih, son of Arphakhsad, son of Shem, son of
Noah, son of Lamek, son of Metushalakh, son of Khanukh, - who, as is believed,
was the prophet Idris, the first prophet, and the first who wrote with the reed, - son
of Yared, son of Mahaleel, son of Kainanan, son of Yanish, son of Sheth, son of
Adam, to whom may God be gracious!
[18] See "The Original Arab, The Bedouin", from the book "The Arabs: A Short
History", Philip K. Hitti, 1996, Regnery Publishing, Inc.
[19] Now a ruins about 215 km northeast of Damascus, Syria.

Arab states bordering the two empires: The Ghassanid Kingdom where Jordan and the eastern part of Syria are today, and the Lakhmid Kingdom, occupying the western part of Iraq and sweeping down to the edges of the Persian Gulf where Kuwait is today. The third kingdom was Yemen, a rival to the Ethiopian Empire[20] that was a Christian kingdom dominating the Horn of Africa and the mouth of the Red Sea. Merchant city states emerged along the trade routes that linked all of these states. The Arab merchant cities included Mecca and Medina. These cities were intermediaries in the trade between India and South Asia and the Roman world, bypassing the Sassanid Kingdom in Persia. The traditional client kingdoms of the Arab world, Ghassanid and Lakhmid[21] were swept away by both the Romans and Sassanids during their epic confrontation in the sixth and early seventh century. That destabilization of the Arab world contributed substantially the subsequent rise of the merchant cities of the Arabian peninsula who occupied the subsequent power vacuum that resulted from the continuous war fought between the two great empires of the Near East, Rome and Persia."

According the Bible, Abraham was an Assyrian from Ur, [22] a Semitic people related to the Arabs and Israelis of today. His birth name was Abram, according to Judeo-Christian beliefs. Abram later in life he

---

[20] Aksum

[21] Prior to the Ghassanid and Lakhmid was the Nabataean Kingdom. Petra was a Nabataean regional capital.

[22] Judeo-Christian beliefs put Ur in South Central Mesopotamia near the southern end of the Fertile Crescent but Islamic beliefs put it at the northern end of the Fertile Crescent, in the hinterlands of the modern day Turkey, Iraq, Syrian borderlands near the Turkish city of Harran.

migrated permanently from his original homeland into Canaan, the modern day region of Israel and Palestine. In the Christian Old Testament and the Hebrew Bible [23] Abram's wife Sarai was considered barren so she offered her Egyptian maid-servant Hagar in order that Abram would not go childless. But after Hagar became pregnant and she began to show signs of jealously and despised Sarai. Sarai then expelled Hagar from Abram's household. Hagar fled into the wilderness, where an angel appeared and promised that her descendants "will be too numerous to count." The angel informed Hagar that she will have a son by Abraham and that his name will be "Ishmael".

I will pass the story to the Book of Genesis, chapter 16.

> "And the angel of the Lord said unto her, Return to thy mistress, and submit thyself unto her hands.
>
> "And the angel of the Lord said unto her, I will multiply thy seed exceedingly that it shall not be numbered by multitude.
>
> "And the angel of the Lord said unto her, Behold, thou art with child, and shalt bear a son, and shalt call his name Ish'ma-el; because the Lord hath heard thy affliction.
>
> "And he will be a wild man; his hand will be against every man, and he shall dwell in the presence of all his brethren." *Genesis 16:10 – 13*

---

[23] See Genesis, Chapter 16

Hagar returned to Abram's household and had a son whom was indeed named Ishmael, meaning "God hears" in Hebrew, who was born in Elonei Mamre ("Oaks of Mamre", or simply "Mamre" in its shorter form). Abram was 86 years old at this time and Ishmael's birth was 11 years after his settling in Canaan. Fourteen years after Ishmael was born, Abram's wife Sarai became pregnant with a son, Isaac. Later in Genesis God made a covenant with Abram[24] when he was 90 years old and changed Abram and Sarai's names to Abraham and Sarah. The name "Abraham" is known as "Ibrahim" to followers of Islam.

Later when Ishmael was around the 16 years old, at a feast held by Abraham to celebrate Isaac's weaning, Ishmael angered Sarah by mocking Isaac. Sarah then demanded that Ishmael and Hagar be cast out from the household into the wilderness. God reassured Abraham that Ishmael would be father of nations as well.[25]

In Islam, Ishmael, or "Ismail" in Arabic, is known as the first-born son of Ibrahim (Abraham) from his second wife Hajar (Hagar to Jews and Christians), as Islamic tradition claims that Ibrahim and Hagar were actually married. The story branches at this point because in the Judeo-Christian background Ishmael had no birthright, whereas in the Muslim tradition Ishmael has a complete birthright as the first born son. Muslims also believe that Ishmael was himself a prophet and was actually the son to have been sacrificed to God but saved by

---

[24] See Genesis, chapter 17
[25] See Genesis, chapter 18

divine intervention (and not Isaac, or Ishaq in Arabic, in the Judeo-Christian belief). As such every year Muslims celebrate Eid ul-Adha to commemorate this. As Ismail is a very highly regarded man in the Quran, Arabs are generally proud to be considered descendants of Ismail.

In the middle part of the first century, 64 BC, the Roman general Pompey conquered Jerusalem. Nearly three decades later, still in the early Roman period, Herod the Great (ruled 37 - 4 BC) of biblical notoriety rebuilt and enlarged the second Temple of Jerusalem and created the famous Wailing Wall, also called the Western Wall and the Wall of Prayer. Many today believe the Wailing Wall to be the last vestige of the Temple of Solomon. This wall was part of the supporting structure for the enlarged Temple Mount.

From 6 AD the Romans administered Jerusalem via a series of procurators. The name of one of these procurators, Pontius Pilate, still lives in infamy as the man ordered the crucifixion of Jesus Christ. Jews twice revolted against their Roman rulers during the next two centuries. And as Alberto Rivera's story alluded, after the quelling of a rebellion in 70 AD, General Titus, who later became the emperor in Rome, destroyed the Second Temple of Jerusalem and banished Jews from living in the city. As Rivera's story this pointed out that Jewish and Christian prophesy was fulfilled.[26]

---

[26] This was not only prophesied in the Book of Matthew, chapter 24. See: Daniel chapter 9, Isaiah chapter 10, Mark chapter 13 and Luke chapter 21. The History of the Church, Eusebius tells that Jerusalem's Christians fled when Cestius Gallus, Rome's legate for Syria, withdrew a full four years before the destruction took

The Jews were only allowed by the Roman rulers to return to the city once per year to mourn their loss. Sixty-five years after the Second Temple's destruction, the Roman Emperor Hadrian, (of Hadrian's wall fame), began construction of a new city, with the Latin name Colonia Aelia Capitolina, in the place that was old Jerusalem and had a temple dedicated to Jupiter on the site of the old Jewish temple. This temple was later demolished as well. Built in its spot was the Church of Holy Zion[27] by the Eastern Roman emperor Constantine I's mother, Empress Helena, visited Jerusalem on a pilgrimage after his conversion to Christianity.

The Dome of the Rock was indeed built on a very sacred and very historical site. The destruction of the temple is only part of the story, somewhere in the middle.

As just mentioned before, during Jerusalem's early Christian era Constantine's mother, Empress Helena, reportedly found the relics of the cross at Golgotha, where Jesus was crucified, at Mount Calvary.[28] In 335 AD, after Helena's visit, the Church of the Holy Sepulchre was built on the site she claimed was that of Christ's Resurrection. This

---

place, whence he lost nearly a legion of soldiers at Beth-Horon. Some secular biblical scholars date the writings of the New Testament after the destruction of the Temple, that the "prophecy" of AD 70 was actually hindsight. Christian scholars dismiss this and point to Old Testament prophesies on the same subject. Jews remained in the vicinity even after the destruction of the Temple. The larger Jewish community in the Middle East however was located to the north near the Sea of Galilee in Safat.

[27] God's Mountain: The Temple Mount in Time, Place, and Memory, Yaron Z. Eliav, Johns Hopkins University Press, 2005

[28] Some believe this to be a fable created for political reasons.

had been the site of a temple dedicated to the worship of Aphrodite.[29] From this time pilgrimages of the early Christians to the holy sites in Jerusalem began and continued uninterrupted until Khusrau I, leader of the Persian Sassanids,[30] invaded early in the seventh century. The Sassanid invasion was welcomed by the Jews and Arian Christians[31] because the East Roman Christian rule had treated them harshly. The Sassanid reign lasted from 614 AD to 638 AD and during their reign the Persians killed many of the citizens, destroyed many Christian shrines and churches and plundered many sacred relics, including the "True Cross", which was not restored to Jerusalem until after Khusrau's assassination ten years later. Their cruelty and brutality can partially be put down to the fact that during this time they were almost constantly at war with Byzantium.

"The Sassanids considered themselves to be successors to the Hellenistic tradition. They tolerated Judaism, Arian Christianity and were formally tied to Zoroastrianism, the state religion of the Persian Empire," explained Len Rosen, "The off and on war fought between the Eastern Roman Empire and the Sassanids started after Justinian's death in 565 AD and continued until Heraclius' improbable campaign in which he invaded the Tigris-Euphrates valley striking into the heart of the Persian Empire in 628 AD. Heraclius, in the restoration of Roman rule, conducted a brutal campaign of repression in Philistia and Judaea-Samaria. If anything the destruction of historical sacred

---

[29] Greek goddess of love, beauty and sexual rapture.
[30] Sassanids were the fourth Iranian dynasty and the last prior to the Arab conquest of Persia.
[31] The Nicene Creed was rejected by several Christian groups, especially in the Eastern Roman Empire.

objects happened in response to the repressive edicts and campaigns of the restored Roman world in the Jerusalem area. It is no wonder that within ten years the people of the area openly welcomed the invasion by their Arab neighbors."

The Arab conqueror who is known to history as Caliph Umar[32] captured Jerusalem in 638 AD and replaced the Byzantine ruler Sophronius. Umar was offered a place to pray in the Church of the Holy Sepulchre by Sophronius, but in order to not begin a precedent of Muslims praying in Christian churches, Umar wasted no time in cleaning the Temple Mount where he built a small mosque called Masjid Al-Aqsa. In the seventh century Arabs, under Abd Al-Malik, built a grand edifice known to us today as "Dome of the Rock" (or in Arabic "Haram Al-Sharif" and "Qubbat As-Sakhrah"). The Dome of the Rock was built on the very location of the two Temples of Jerusalem and the descendant Temple of Jupiter. This glorious structure was built on this spot in order to insure Muslims would not be tempted by Christianity and as well to show the supremacy of Islam. The Dome of the Rock was built very near the Church of the Holy Sepulchre and the Wailing Wall. Unlike what Alberto Rivera has claimed though, the Dome of the Rock is not Islam's second most holy sites. Muslims consider the Dome of the Rock and Al-Aqsa Mosque as one site alone, Al-Aqsa being a mosque and the Dome of the Rock being a shrine for Muslim pilgrims, or known in Islam as a "mashhad". Together this site consisting of both Al-Aqsa and the

---

[32] Caliph Umar (c. 581 AD – 644 AD) is known in the Arab and Muslim worlds as "Umar Ibn Al-Khattab" and also "Umar Al-Faruq".

Dome of the Rock is the third most holy site in Islam after Al-Kaaba in Mecca and the Prophet's Mosque in Medina.

There were other reasons that the Dome of the Rock was built in this location. One reason was politically related and had to do with a power struggle between the powers that be in Mecca and the Umayyad Caliphate.[33] But the other main reason was religious.

Faithful Muslims believe also that Mohammed himself was brought to this location in a night journey by the Archangel Jabril (Gabriel) riding on the back of a winged equestrian creature called "Al-Burak",[34] stopping first at Mount Sinai and Bethlehem before coming to the pinnacle of the Temple Mount in Jerusalem, known in Arabic as "As-Sakhra". Here a Mohammed met many prophets including Ibrahim (Abraham), Jesus (Issa), Musa (Moses) and others, whom Mohammed led in prayer. Afterwards a ladder of light appeared on which Mohammed ascended to the heavens to the presence of Allah where he received instructions. Upon Mohammed receiving the instructions, Jabril flew him back to Mecca before daybreak.

Regarding Alberto Rivera's "sweeping changes" that were "in the wind" and all the vices that were causing the end of the Roman Empire, as it turns out he was completely and utterly off the mark by centuries. In 476 AD, the Western part of the Roman Empire was

---

[33] The Umayyad Dynasty was the first dynasty of caliphs of the Islamic empire after the end of the reign of the Four Rightly Guided Caliphs (Abu Bakr, Umar, Uthman, and Ali).

[34] Arabic for "lightning".

lost, but the Eastern part continued until 1453 AD as the Eastern Roman Empire, which is now more often referred to as the Byzantine Empire,[35] with Constantinople as its capital. Rivera was unclear as to what date he was referring to when he declared the Roman Empire was "ready to collapse". From the way the text is written he alludes to 70 AD. If that was the case Alberto Rivera was over 400 years off from the fall of the Western Roman Empire and almost 1400 years off from the fall of the Eastern Roman Empire. If Alberto Rivera was actually referring to the "end of the third century" when the Roman Catholics, according to Rivera, had hatched the scheme to "make Jerusalem a Roman Catholic city", again he'd be nearly 200 years from the fall of the Western Roman Empire and around 1180 years or so from the fall of the Eastern Roman Empire. Either way this part of the testimony is looked at, Alberto Rivera's claims were unsubstantiated.

---

[35] And even simply "Byzantium" as Constantinople had been known.

The Birth of Catholicism

"The only way Satan could stop this thrust was to create a counterfeit 'Christian' religion to destroy the work of God. The solution was in Rome. Their religion had come from ancient Babylon and all it needed was a face-lift. This didn't happen overnight, but began in the writings of the 'early church fathers'.

"It was through their writings that a new religion would take shape. The statue of Jupiter in Rome was eventually called St. Peter, and the statue of Venus was changed to the Virgin Mary. The site chosen for its headquarters was on one of the seven hills called 'Vaticanus', the place of the diving serpent where the Satanic temple of Janus stood.

"The great counterfeit religion was Roman Catholicism, called 'Mystery, Babylon the Great, the Mother of Harlots and Abominations of the Earth'-Revelation 17:5. She was raised up to block the gospel, slaughter the believers in Christ, establish religions, create wars and make the nations drunk with the wine of her fornication as we will see.

The Prophet, by Jack T. Chick, Chick Publications, 1988

Alberto Rivera's first assertion regarding Satan, or Jack Chick's assertion as it may well be, is very much give or take. You either believe it or you don't. Personally I cannot.

Why?

48

One must use a common sense rule of thumb when discussing such broad supernatural generalities as Satan's power, Satan's knowledge, and Satan's reach. It doesn't make sense to me that an entity powerful enough to be considered an adversary of God as far as mankind is concerned, an evil supernatural being with armies of demons at his beck and call who has permission from God to tempt mankind, would be limited of options for swaying man away from God. And I also personally believe that Satan is unfathomable to man's mind because Satan is an entity unlike any that we can sense on earth. We simply cannot know Satan's true nature and only can know Satan's characteristics by what has been revealed to us in the Bible. We can easily see what we believe is the work of Satan on earth but we cannot easily see the extent of Satan's capability. Only God almighty and Satan can truly have this knowledge.

Again, the above comments about Satan are strictly my opinion. I base this on belief only, so therefore all I am saying with this part of Rivera's statement is that I cannot believe Alberto Rivera on this point. I also believe Rivera would never be able to prove that Satan had only one way to stop the early Christians. (What of the virtually universal persecutions suffered by early Christians?)

Nevertheless, again the tract returns to focus on Rome as a Church center. We have already established in my preceding arguments that there was no central universal church during the third century. There were many church centers with budding churches spoken of in the New Testament. Some examples are Ephesus, Corinth, Thessalonia, etc. But N.S. Dill, a writer and specialist on Ancient History who studied the Classics at the University of Chicago and at the University of Minnesota, tells us by the time of the birth of Islam Rome was definitely not alone in the leadership of the Christendom. "There were five Apostolic Sees,"[36] said Dill, "The Church was not yet divided, except by heresies, producing things like the Nestorian churches." And Dill is in agreement with Ralph Williams regarding the Eastern Churches having been stronger than Rome in the earlier years, especially after the Christian Church's official legalization. "If anything, I imagine Constantine would likely have followed the See at Constantinople rather than the one at Rome," she said.

In the early Church there were five major centers with budding congregations, or *Sees*, of Christianity. These five Sees are known as the Apostolic Sees because they were said to have been founded by the apostles of Jesus.

Rivera then states that the statues of Jupiter and Venus were converted to statues of Saint Peter and the Virgin Mary. This is possible given that the Roman Catholic Church very often found it easier to convert pagans to Christianity when they used cultural icons that pagans were familiar and comfortable with. But more on this later…

---

[36] The word "See" comes from the Latin "sedes", which means seat (of power). By tradition, the Sees at Rome and at Antioch (in Syria) were said to have been established by Peter; the See at Constantinople (Byzantium) by Andrew; the See at Alexandria (Egypt) by Mark; and the See at Jerusalem by James. All were thus apostolic patriarchates. The Patriarchate of Antioch moved to Damascus during the rule of the Egyptian Mamelukes. It remains there today.

Such statue conversions may also have been expediency or out of official preservation of art. I have been able to find only one list of statue conversions but have not been able to find any back up information for these conversions to know whether they actually happened or not. According to E. Cobham Brewer.:

Pagan Works of Art.

In Rome there are numerous works of art intended for Pagan deities and Roman emperors perverted into Christian notabilities.

ANGELS, in St. Peter's of Rome, are old Pagan statues of Cupids and winged genii.
GABRIEL, in St. Peter's of Rome, is an old Pagan statue of the god Mercury.
JOHN THE BAPTIST, in St. Peter's of Rome, is made out of a statue of Hercules.
ST. CATHERINE, in St. Peter's of Rome, is made out of a statue of the goddess Fortna.
ST. GILES (or EGIDIUS), in St. Peter's of Rome, is a statue of Vulcan.
ST. PAUL. Sixtus V. perverted the original statue of Marcus Aurlius Antonnus into that of St. Paul. This beautiful marble column, 170 feet in height, contains a spiral of bas-reliefs of the wars of the Roman emperor, wholly out of character with the statue which surmounts it.
ST. PETER. The same Pope (Sixtus V.) converted the original statue of Trajan, on Trajan's column, into a statue of St. Peter. This exquisite column, like that of Antonnus, contains a spiral of bas-reliefs, representing the wars of Trajan. Surmounted by St. Peter, the perversion is absolutely ludicrous. In St. Peter's of Rome the statue of St. Peter was meant for the old Roman god Jupiter.

VIRGIN MARY. This statue, in St. Peter's of Rome, is in reality a statue of Isis, standing on the crescent Moon.[37]

Again, I am not to saying that these above conversions and even numerous others both in Rome and in other locations throughout the Roman Empire did happen or did not happen. I believe it was probable but my research is inconclusive for lack of fully reliable sources at my disposal.

Backing up a bit in the Rivera story we find that Alberto Rivera makes claims that the Roman Catholic religion was simply the religion of ancient Babylon in disguise. Let's look into that, beginning by looking first at the Church of the Chaldeans (also known as Assyrians and Aramaic people), the direct descendants of the ancient Babylonians.

Dr. Farouq Dawood, a Chaldean Church priest from Iraq who was also an author, having written 26 books and served as the dean of Iraq's Babylon College for Philosophy and Liturgy, believed that the Christianity of the Church of the East, (Chaldean Church, Assyrian Church), itself did incorporate some of Mesopotamia's ancient culture into its beliefs. He felt that this was an unavoidable osmosis that was unwanted by the early Church fathers.

---

[37] Dictionary of Phrase and Fable, John Ayto (Editor), Cassell Reference; 17 Rev Edition, 2005. Originally written and published by E. Cobham Brewer (1810–1897), 1898

"Belonging to a certain identity changes from one era to another, example, when Christianity spread, especially in our East, it tried somehow to distance the people from their old heritage, since it considered it as based on idol worshipping. However, part of the old heritage stayed and that was unavoidable, especially, beliefs and literature. Those stayed all the way.

"The civilization of the land between the two rivers, Mesopotamia, the old Iraqi civilization, it's not only a well known civilization, but everyone knows it was the first civilization in the world. It started with the Sumerian, Akkadian, Babylonian, and then the Assyrian. Writing was invented in this land. Add to that record-keeping and literature, and we have great epics. Some epics were adopted by Christianity as stories. Take for the example the story of Mar Gorgees, or Jarjees or George. This story is originally a Sumerian epic. This epic of the killing of the dragon. Mar Gorgees or Jarjees or George, this martyr was added to this epic and was made to fight the dragon, while the original story is Sumerian. It's a nice and symbolic story. Also, the monastic impressions that we see in the Epic of Gilgamesh, it continued in the Chaldean, Assyrian, Syriac Church of the East. That is when we talk about our spiritual Fathers like Is-Haq Al Ninevehi, Youhanna Dalyathi. Even among Sufi Muslims, they got close to those areas, for they always considered God as too lofty for man to ever reach. Man can reach the water of the stream, but cannot dive in it, i.e., cannot dive in the meaning of God's self.

"In other words, the Eastern, whether Chaldean, Assyrian or Arab or whatever the name is, managed to preserve his civilizational characteristics as well as heritage and history throughout times. Religion was not able, if I may say, to sever those belongings; attachment to the land, to history, and attachment to the civilization in general and that was a positive thing in my opinion. Religion, for sure, did not come to cut off, but to add on. However, when religions increased in variety as they did in the past, when Christianity started to spread, the majority of the people were believers in their idol-worshipping religions. The new religious regimes, of course, at the beginning they had differences with this old society, but they could not nor they wanted to distance themselves 100% from their civilization's heritage, from their linguistic heritage, etc. But this happened many years later after the coming of Islam to the country."[38]

This Chaldean Church, the Church of the East, is not the Roman Catholic Church though, and it should be noted again that the Church of the East is a Nestorian church[39] which was considered heretical by both the Roman Catholic and Eastern Orthodox Churches from the Nestorian schism in 431 AD until late twentieth century in 1994 when the patriarch of the Church of the East, Mar Dinkha IV, met with pope John Paul II, to sign the Common Christological Declaration.

In 1552 AD, after a split concerning patriarchal succession, one group of the Chaldean Church broke ranks and began communion with the Roman Catholic Church. About 110 years later, this splinter group split again with some members rejoining the Church of the East and some churches remaining in communion with the Roman Catholic Church.[40] The group which stayed in communion with Rome became known as the Chaldean Catholic Church, or also the Chaldean Church

---

[38] "Chaldeans of Iraq: Past and Present", Interview of Fr. Yousif Habbi, Al Jazeera, Broadcasted on November 5th, 2000. Yousif Habbi was the pen name Dr. Farouq Dawood used.

[39] An Introduction To The History Of The Assyrian Church, William Wigram, Gorgias Press, 2004

[40] The Eastern Catholic Churches: An Introduction to Their Worship and Spirituality, Joan L. Roccasalvo, Liturgical Press, 1992

of Babylon. It is an eastern rite autonomous church within the Roman Catholic Church. The name "Babylon" in the Church's name relates to the Babylonian origins of the Chaldean people and not a specific religious creed that is derived from Babylonian sources.

Father Felix Al-Shabi, an Iraqi Chaldean who studied Canonical Law of the Eastern Churches at the Pontifical Oriental Institute at the Vatican and serves as the parochial vicar of the Saint Peter Chaldean Catholic Cathedral in San Diego, California, affirms that the Babylonian theology was not transferred to Roman Catholic theology. "The Roman empire never reached the borders of the Babylonian empire," said Father Al-Shabi, "Mesopotamia at the Roman time was occupied by the Persian Empire.[41] From a religious point of view, Christianity was born in Israel, and the disciples went out from Jerusalem to Antioch first, then to Asia Minor and later to the rest of the world. Thus there is no connection between our Babylonian culture and the Roman Catholic culture at all."

Throughout the Roman Catholic faith one is able to find traces of the former pagan religions in Catholic practices such as holy water, lifting of the host, processions, prayers for the dead, votive offerings, etc.[42] Some of these traces are localized to regions and some are permeated

---

[41] This is true because Babylon was a dead empire by the time the Romans came to Mesopotamia. The Roman Empire actually did conquer Mesopotamia and Assyria in 116 AD which under the Emperor Trajan. By Trajan's death the following year much of southern Mesopotamia was already lost. Trajan's rule marked the geographical high water mark of the Roman Empire. But Babylon as a city and political entity ended in 275 AD, which is 391 years before Trajan's conquest.
[42] Survivals of Roman Religion (Our Debt to Greece and Rome Series), Gordon J. Laing, Cooper Square Pub, 1960

throughout the Church's tradition. This is not an uncommon phenomenon that has only occurred in Catholicism. Many of these tenants have made it directly into Protestantism and Western culture as well. Some good examples are Sunday worship,[43] exchanging of wedding rings, the celebration of Christmas in December, etc. Franz Cumont tells us that some of these pagan rituals of Semitic origin found their way into daily Roman culture through their rule of Syriac lands. Aurelian, the Roman emperor who conquered Palmyra in what is today eastern Syria raised "Sol Invictus", the Mithraists' invincible sun god, to the ranks of supreme divinity in the Empire.[44] During this time the Romans did absorb certain myths and deities into their religion from conquered peoples in Syria, Palestine and Egypt, just as they had when they conquered the Greeks. Some of the more popular gods that found their way to Rome were Isis and Ishtar, yet still the Greco-Roman religions, with the exception of the Persian Mithraism which was quite strong from the first to the fifth centuries,[45] held sway over other pagan traditions.

Mithraism, which probably began about 4000 years ago in eastern Persia, was an ancient religion that centered around worship of the god Mithras, or Mithra. Mithraist beliefs, festivals and traditions did

---

[43] See: Semitic (Mythology of All Races, Volume V), Stephen H. Langdon, Cooper Square Pub, 1932; and
Sun Lore of All Ages : A Collection of Myths and Legends, William Tyler Olcott, Dover Publications, 2005
[44] Oriental Religions in Roman Paganism, Franz Cumont, Wipf & Stock Publishers, 2003. It is also worthy to note that Aurelian's mother was a priestess who believed in sun worship.
[45] Roman Society from Nero to Marcus Aurelius, Samuel Dill, Kessinger Publishing, 2003

make it directly into the Greco-Roman and Babylonian cultures,[46] but it is important to note that Mithraism did not come to Rome via ancient Babylon, which was long extinct as an empire by the time Mithraism made it to Europe. The religion is thought to most likely have come to Rome via Roman soldiers returning from Armenia during the second half of the first century, from which it soon spread from Dacia to the British Isles to the Iberian Peninsula and all throughout the Roman Empire. In fact, Alberto Rivera's claims that the Vatican was built on "the place of the diving serpent where the satanic temple of Janus stood" is factually untrue. The Vatican sits on the site where Mithra's cave temple stood. This temple was seized in 376 AD by Christians.[47] As a result the word now used for "pope" comes indirectly from this take over of Mithra's temple. Mithra's high priest was in the days prior to his disposal was called "Pater Patrum", which later Bishop's of Rome took.[48] This name was later shortened in Latin to "papa" by using the first two syllables of "Pater Patrum", which is where we ultimately get the word "pope" in English.

This absorption of pagan rites and traditions into Roman Catholicism was partly a natural step very similar to what Dr. Farouq Dawood described in the Church of the East. Part of this was unavoidable. The Church was taking on the cultures of the new believers, who in turn, changed many facets of the Church. The historian and

---

[46] Ancient Mystery Cults, Walter Burkert, Harvard University Press, 1987
[47] The Death of Classical Paganism, John Holland Smith, G. Chapman, 1976
[48] Man and his Gods, Homer William Smith, Little, Brown, 1952. In the sixth century Pope Gregory I was the first pope to officially use this title for himself.

philosopher Will Durant described these Catholic borrowings from paganism and the changing shape of the Church as follows:

> "The belief in miracle-working objects, talismans, amulets, and formulas was dear to Christianity, and they were received from pagan antiquity… The vestments of the clergy and the papal title of 'pontifex maximus' were legacies from pagan Rome. The [Catholic] Church found that rural converts still revered certain springs, wells, trees, and stones; she thought it wiser to bless these to Christian use than to break too sharply the customs of sentiment… Pagan festivals dear to the people, reappeared as Christian feasts, and pagan rites were transformed into Christian liturgy… The Christian calendar of saints replaced the Roman 'fasti' [gods]; ancient divinities dear to the people were allowed to revive under the names of 'Christian saints'… Gradually the tenderest features of Astarte, Cybele, Artemis, Diana, and Isis were gathered together in the worship of Mary".[49]

Later in his monumental work, "An Essay on the Development of Christian Doctrine", John Henry Newman, later Cardinal Newman, gave a good example of how Saint Gregory Thaumaturgus used paganistic festivals of the dead, but instead honoring the dead Christian martyrs to focus early Christians on God in lieu of paganism.

> "Confiding then in the power of Christianity to resist the infection of evil, and to transmute the very instruments and appendages of demon-worship to an

---

[49] The Age of Faith: A History of Medieval Civilization - Christian, Islamic, and Judaic - from Constantine to Dante: A.D. 325-1300, Will Durant, Simon & Schuster, 1950

evangelical use, and feeling also that these usages had originally come from primitive revelations and from the instinct of nature, though they had been corrupted; and that they must invent what they needed, if they did not use what they found; and that they were moreover possessed of the very archetypes, of which paganism attempted the shadows; the rulers of the Church from early times were prepared, should the occasion arise, to adopt, or imitate, or sanction the existing rites and customs of the populace, as well as the philosophy of the educated class.

"St. Gregory Thaumaturgus supplies the first instance on record of this economy. He was the Apostle of Pontus, and one of his methods for governing an untoward population is thus related by St. Gregory of Nyssa. 'On returning,' he says, 'to the city, after revisiting the country round about, he increased the devotion of the people everywhere by instituting festive meetings in honour of those who had fought for the faith. The bodies of the Martyrs were distributed in different places, and the people assembled and made merry, as the year came round, holding festival in their honour. This indeed was a proof of his great wisdom ... for, perceiving that the childish and untrained populace were retained in their idolatrous error by creature comforts, in order that what was of first importance should at any rate be secured to them, viz. that they should look to God in place of their vain rites, he allowed them to be merry, jovial, and gay at the monuments of the holy Martyrs, as if their behaviour would in time undergo a spontaneous change into greater seriousness and strictness, since faith would lead them to it; which has actually been the happy issue in that population, all carnal gratification having turned into a spiritual form of rejoicing."[50]

---

[50] An Essay on the Development of Christian Doctrine, John Henry Cardinal Newman, Wipf & Stock, 2005. Newman wrote this while he was still an Anglican clergyman and was yet to join the Catholic Church but well after the beginning of

Many latter day Catholic apologists and clergy have carried the same view as Cardinal Newman but saw this as a good doctrinal tool for winning converts and keeping them converted.[51] But this Roman Catholic usurping of various local paganistic rituals does not make the religion that the Roman Catholics follow to be a paganistic cult any more than it makes Christian brides of any denomination pagans for getting married in white bridal gowns and wearing a wedding ring, two traditions which also have their roots in pagan religions. The basic theology of Roman Catholicism, which that religion must be judged on, is anti-pagan and has been since the beginning. If someone is worshipping Mary, whether that act has its roots in worshiping Isis, Venus, Ishtar, Astarte, or any other deity, it does not take anything away from the basic fact that the intended object of worship is specifically Mary herself. The Catholic does not believe he or she is praying to anyone else. Whether the Protestant agrees with that statement is inconsequential. In this statement Alberto Rivera falsely claims that Roman Catholicism comes from the ancient Babylonian religion. The truth in a nutshell is that Roman Catholicism developed over nearly two millennia and was duly influenced by many other religions, but its roots were in early Christian teachings, not Babylon theology.

Further to the assertion by Alberto Rivera that the Vatican was actually built on one of Rome's seven hills, known as "Vaticanus", is

---

the Oxford Movement, which sought to bring the Church of England back to its Catholic Roots.
[51] Faith of Our Fathers, James Cardinal Gibbons, TAN Books & Publishers, 1980

also a fallacy. The Vatican is not even on the same side of the Tiber River as the Seven Hills of Rome.[52] The location of the Vatican was known in Latin as "Mons Vaticanus" since pre-Christian times and was most likely an old Etruscan village prior to the Latinization of the area. The hill that the Vatican sits on was not even part of the city of Rome until the late ninth century. Vatican City, the sovereign polis, again has not been technically part of Rome, but an independent nation since the signing of the Lateran Treaties in 1929,[53] in which the Italy formally recognized Vatican City as an independent state which is the heir of the former Papal States.

Also Rivera, not unlike a great many other evangelicals, jumps to an automatic conclusion that the "Mystery, Babylon the Great, the Mother of Harlots and Abominations of the Earth" personage in the New Testament's Book of Revelation must absolutely be Rome, but this is extremely speculative. Some scholars have in the past even thought the city mentioned in the Book of Revelation is Jerusalem, another historical and religiously important city with seven hills. To be sure, should we count the hills in Salt Lake City, Istanbul, Avignon, or Canterbury? How about Mexico City, Cape Town, Zurich or Varanasi for that matter?

---

[52] The Seven Hills of Rome are: Aventine Hill, Caelian Hill, Capitoline Hill, Esquiline Hill, Palatine Hill, Quirinal Hill, and Viminal Hill.
[53] The Treaty of the Lateran, Benedict Williamson, Burns, Oates & Washbourne, 1929

The Chosen One

"Three major religions have one thing in common - each has a holy place where they look for guidance. Roman Catholicism looks to the Vatican as the Holy City. The Jews look to the Wailing Wall [sic] in Jerusalem, and the Muslims look to Mecca as their Holy City. Each group believes that they receive certain types of blessings for the rest of their lives for visiting their holy place. In the beginning, Arab visitors would bring gifts to the 'House of God', and the keepers of the Kaaba were gracious to all who came. Some brought their idols and, not wanting to offend these people, their idols were placed inside the sanctuary. It is said that the Jews looked upon the Kaaba as an outlying tabernacle of the Lord with veneration until it became polluted with idols."

"In a tribal contention over a well (Zamzam) the treasure of the Kaaba and the offerings that pilgrims had given were dumped down the well and it was filled with sand - it disappeared. Many years later Adb Al-Muttalib was given visions telling him where to find the well and its treasure. He became the hero of Mecca, and he was destined to become the grandfather of Muhammad. Before this time, Augustine became the bishop of North Africa and was effective in winning Arabs to Roman Catholicism, including whole tribes. It was among these Arab converts to Catholicism that the concept of looking for an Arab prophet developed.

"Muhammad's father died from illness and sons born to great Arab families in places like Mecca were sent into the desert to be suckled and weaned and spend some of their childhood with Bedouin tribes for training and to avoid the plagues in the cities.

"After his mother and grandfather also died, Muhammad was with his uncle when a Roman Catholic monk learned of his identity and said, "Take your brother's son back to his country and guard him against the Jews, for by god, if they see him and know of him that which I know, they will construe evil against him. Great things are in store for this brother's son of yours."

"The Roman Catholic monk had fanned the flames for future Jewish persecutions at the hands of the followers of Muhammad. The Vatican desperately wanted Jerusalem because of its religious significance, but was blocked by the Jews.

The Prophet, by Jack T. Chick, Chick Publications, 1988

Rivera's first claim was not 100% off the mark and not 100% bull's eye either. While it is true that many believers of Islam, Catholicism and Judaism feel that they will get blessings for their pilgrimages, this is not necessarily true in all cases. For instance, Muslims should complete a hajj, pilgrimage to Mecca, during their life time if they are physically and financially able. But this doesn't automatically bestow a blessing. "Muslims believe they are getting a lot of blessings by visiting Mecca, doing hajj or umra" explains Imam Dr. Yusuf Ziya Kavakci of the Islamic Association of North Texas, "We don't qualify this blessing as 'certain'."

What is certain is what the pilgrims receive from the experience. Adam Harmon, an American Jew who served in the Israeli armed forces puts it this way.

"Being a Jew, the idea of Jerusalem and of Israel is a central part of our religion, of all of our holidays, and our prayers. Before I went there, it was sort of an abstract place. But when I went there, what changed was that I felt really connected to it. When we went to the [Western or "Wailing"] Wall, I realized that this wall has been here thousands of years, and my ancestors prayed here. It presented a real emotional connection between my distant past and my people, and showed me how I was a part of that. The idea of actually wanting to live there grew out of that first experience."[54]

Referring to the Quran, the Kaaba[55] in Mecca was built by the Ibrahim (Abraham) and Ismail (Ishmael). Mohammed's own tribe was in charge of the Kaaba during Mohammed's time. During Mohammed's early years, prior to his revelations, the Kaaba was a shrine to numerous gods represented in the Kaaba by idols. Even during this time, Mecca was the site for annual pilgrimages by Arabs.

Although Rivera's claim regarding the Jews worshipping in the Kaaba would be very difficult to substantiate, it may also not be unlikely. Reza Aslan puts it this way:

"Although in contact with major Jewish centers throughout the Near East, Judaism in Arabia had developed its own variations on traditional Jewish beliefs and practices. The Jews shared many of the same religious ideals as their pagan Arab counterparts,

---

[54] "3000-Year Recon: An American in the Israeli Army", by Mike Milliard, The Phoenix Newsletter, July 5th, 2006
[55] Per Islamic tradition, Allah set aside a place of worship on Earth to mirror the house in heaven, Al-Baytu l-Ma'mur. Adam was the first to build such a place, according to Islam.

especially with regard to what is sometimes referred to as 'popular religion': belief in magic, the use of talismans and divination, and the like. For example, while there is evidence of a small yet formal rabbinical presence in some regions of the Arabian Peninsula, there also existed a group of Jewish soothsayers called the Kohens who, while maintaining a far more priestly function in their communities, nevertheless resembled the pagan Kahins in that they too dealt in divinely inspired oracles.

"The relationship between the Jews and pagan Arabs was symbiotic in that not only were the Jews heavily arabized, but the Arabs were also significantly influenced by Jewish beliefs and practices. One need look no further for evidence of this influence than to the Kaaba itself, whose origin myths indicate that it was a Semitic sanctuary (haram in Arabic) with its roots dug deeply in Jewish tradition. Adam, Noah, Abraham, Moses, and Aaron were all in one way or another associated with the Kaaba long before the rise of Islam, and the mysterious Black Stone that to this day is fixed to the southeast corner of the sanctuary seems to have been originally associated with the same stone upon which Jacob rested his head during his famous dream of the ladder."[56]

Islamic tradition provides that that Well of Zamzam[57] mentioned by Alberto Rivera was revealed to Hajar (Hagar),[58] the wife of Ibrahim (Abraham). Hajar was desperately seeking water for her small son Ishmael yet could find none. Jews and Christians have a related story in Genesis, chapter 21.:

---

[56] No God But God: The Origins, Evolution, and Future of Islam, Reza Aslan, Random House, 2005
[57] The Well of Zamzam is a well in the Masjid al Haram in Mecca, near the Kaaba, which is the holiest place in Islam.
[58] The Meaning Of The Holy Quran, Abdullah Yusuf Ali, Amana Publications, 2004

"And God opened her eyes, and she saw a well of
water; and she went, and filled the bottle with water,
and gave the lad drink." Genesis 21:19

Rivera mentioned that Abdul Muttalib, (Rivera got the name wrong),
found the Well of Zamzam and its treasure, making him the "hero of
Mecca". Well, close, but it didn't really happen so simply…

Generations later, after the Well of Zamzam had been filled with
sand, Abdul Muttalib,[59] Mohammed's paternal grandfather,
rediscovered this well and became its guardian. This was no well that
Abdul Muttalib just "happened upon".

Tradition has it that Abdul Muttalib had a series of four dreams
directing him to the location. He and his eldest son, Harith ibn Abd
Al-Muttalib, found the location. They finally uncovered the well after
four days of work. The Quraysh tribe claimed the well belonged to
the whole tribe because the well had originally belonged to Ismail but
Abdul Muttalib refused, claiming that Allah had given the well
directly to him. In order to settle the dispute they agreed to travel to
Syria to let a woman who was respected for her wisdom made the
decision. In the meantime while crossing the desert, they all,
including Abdul Muttalib, ran out of water. The morning after
exhorting the members of the party to begin digging graves for one
another Abdul Muttalib mounted a camel declaring that it was

---

[59] Shaiba ibn Hashim (c. 497 AD – 578 AD) was his correct name but he was raised
by his uncle Muttalib, thus he was more widely known as "Abdul Muttalib", or
"Slave of Muttalib", because many locals thought Shaiba to be a slave.

cowardice to just let death come and take them. His camel's hoof then struck a stream of water. The Qurayshi took this as a sign that Zamzam was rightfully the well of Abdul Muttalib.[60]

Again at this point Alberto Rivera repeats his false claim about Arabs being all over North Africa and having been converted to Roman Catholicism, which has been disproved in previous chapters. Also, Saint Augustine, it should be pointed out, was not the "Bishop of North Africa", but rather the "Bishop of Hippo Regius",[61] or simply the "Bishop of Hippo". It should be noted that North Africa had numerous Christian bishops, beginning with the city of Alexandria in Egypt. Rivera also ignores the very important fact that the distance between Hippo and Mecca is approximately the same as the distance from modern day Ankara, Turkey, to London. And virtually all of the way being difficult desert. Again, keeping in mind this is at a time period when travel of great distances was extremely slow and also the fact that Arabs did not populate North Africa then.

Abd-Allah ibn Abd-Al-Muttalib, Mohammed's father, died even before Mohammed's birth. The year that both Mohammed's mother and grandfather died, Mohammed went to live with his uncle, Abu

---

[60] Secular scholars find these stories highly doubtful historically speaking, but many believe that Zamzam might well have been important commercially to the pre-Islamic inhabitants of Mecca. It may be an early impetus to Mecca's future as a pilgrimage center.

[61] Hippo Regius, or Hippo, is the ancient Roman name for the modern day city now called Annabas, which is in eastern Algeria near the Tunisian border.

Talib.[62] It was during one of his journeys to Syria with his uncle that the monk or priest Bahira made his appearance in Islamic tradition.

"The Prophet Mohammad met a priest, a Christian one when he was traveling Syria, his name was Bahira, but I am not sure he was Catholic or some other denomination priest," explains Imam Kavakci, "Orientalists claim a lot of influence from him [Bahira] on young Mohammad, but we Muslims believe that his meeting Mohammad was not that extraordinary or anything. Christians and Jews and polytheists Arabs were around, everywhere that time. Islam was not even begun to flourish yet that time. We don't believe Muhammad took his education or got knowledge from a priest or Jew, or Gospels or Torah, etc. We believe he was ummi,[63] not trained and educated by no one, he was as he was born on the religion of Abraham, natural religion, hanif,[64] as it is mentioned in Quran."

Other sources are a bit more detailed about Bahira. According to Thomas Patrick Hughes, a nineteenth century clergyman who was also an expert on Islamic studies.:

"Bahira is a Nestorian monk that Muhammad was supposed to have met during a trip returning from Syria to Mecca. His Christian name was supposed to be Sergius or Georgius. The Muslim traditions say that Bahira recognized, through various signs, that Muhammad is a

---

[62] Abu Talib was leader of the Hashim clan of the Quraysh tribe, the most powerful in Mecca.
[63] "Ummi" means "unlettered" in Arabic.
[64] A pre-Islamic monotheist, one who rejected idols.

prophet. There are suggestions that Bahira stayed with Muhammad and taught him as alluded to in Surah xvi.105. 'Husain the commentator says on this passage that the Prophet was in the habit of going every evening to a Christian to hear the Taurat and Injil.'"[65]

Karen Armstrong, a well known biographer of Mohammed, backs this up.:

> "In the civilized lands, many of the Arabs had converted to Christianity and in the fourth century had formed their own distinctive Syriac church.[66] But in general the Bedouin Arabs of Arabia Deserta were suspicious of both Judaism and Christianity, even though they realized that both these religions were more sophisticated than their own."[67]

As the extremely high likelihood was that Bahira was indeed actually a Nestorian, which most Christians of that region were, or an Arian, which would also have been much more likely than having been a Roman Catholic, then there is no way that there would have been any connection with Saint Augustine, who was already separated by time and distance, let alone religious doctrine. Again, by the time of Mohammed, Saint Augustine had been dead for centuries, had lived extremely far traveling distance away for those times. It also doesn't seem prudent that Saint Augustine would not have used a heretic to

---

[65] A Dictionary of Islam : Being a Cyclopaedia of the Doctrines, Rites, Ceremonies and Customs, Together With the Technical and Theological Terms, of the Muslim Religion, Thomas Patrick Hughes, Kazi Publications, 1994

[66] The Syriac Church was known as Church of the East, still surviving today as the world's major Nestorian denomination.

[67] Muhammad: A Biography of the Prophet, Karen Armstrong, Phoenix Press, 1991

spread his teachings, especially since Saint Augustine spoke in favor of a just war against the heretic Donatists.

Regarding the "warning" against Jews, this is not within Islamic tradition. Even contemporary modern accounts mention that Abu Talib was warned to take care of the "orphan" because of his future greatness, but there are no accounts that warn Abu Talib of Jews.[68] Again, Alberto Rivera missed the mark.

---

[68] "The Orphan's Childhood", Arab News Newspaper, by an unattributed author, July 6th, 2006

Khadijah

"Another problem was the true Christians in North Africa who preached the gospel. Roman Catholicism was growing in power, but would not tolerate opposition. Somehow the Vatican had to create a weapon to eliminate both the Jews and the true Christian believers who refused to accept Roman Catholicism. Looking to North Africa, they saw the multitudes of Arabs as a source of manpower to do their dirty work. Some Arabs had become Roman Catholic, and could be used in reporting information to leaders in Rome. Others were used in an underground spy network to carry out Rome's master plan to control the great multitudes of Arabs who rejected Catholicism. When 'St Augustine' appeared on the scene, he knew what was going on. His monasteries served as bases to seek out and destroy Bible manuscripts owned by the true Christians.

"The Vatican wanted to create a messiah for the Arabs, someone they could raise up as a great leader, a man with charisma whom they could train, and eventually unite all the non-Catholic Arabs behind him, creating a mighty army that would ultimately capture Jerusalem for the pope. In the Vatican briefing, Cardinal Bea told us this story:

'A wealthy Arabian lady who was a faithful follower of the pope played a tremendous part in this drama. She was a widow named Khadijah. She gave her wealth to the church and retired to a convent, but was given an assignment. She was to find a brilliant young man who could be used by the Vatican to create a new religion and become the messiah for the children of Ishmael. Khadijah had a cousin named Waraquah, who was also a very faithful Roman Catholic and the Vatican placed him in a critical role as Muhammad's advisor. He had tremendous influence on Muhammad.

'Teachers were sent to young Muhammad and he had intensive training. Muhammad studied the works of St. Augustine which prepared him for his "great calling." The Vatican had Catholic Arabs across North Africa spread the story of a great one who was about to rise up among the people and be the chosen one of their God.

'While Muhammad was being prepared, he was told that his enemies were the Jews and that the only true Christians were Roman Catholic. He was taught that others calling themselves Christians were actually wicked impostors and should be destroyed. Many Muslims believe this.
The Prophet, by Jack T. Chick, Chick Publications, 1988

First of all, as we have said before there were not any multitudes of Arabs in North Africa during this time as Alberto Rivera so claimed. But to drive the point further home I will now elaborate on what groups of people were populating North Africa at the time.

The main societies of the North Africans were the native Egyptians, who are now known as Copts (in Egypt all along the Nile River and the Nile Delta), the Punic descendants of the Phoenicians and Carthaginians (Carthage, which had homelands and colonies extended from Libya, Tunisia, and Algeria and even stretched all the way to Morocco), Berbers on the Sahara with a few Berbers dwelling and trading in the cities, Romans (mainly soldiers, merchants and administrators), and Greeks who were descendants both of Greeks who had established colonies since the earliest of times as well as contemporary Greeks who came with the Roman and Byzantine Empires. There were other much smaller minorities as well who would have come from other parts of the Roman and Byzantine Empires and also from deeper into the African continent. The Arabs who did exist in North Africa did not get much further than eastern Egypt and had been mainly traveling traders. They were not settlers. There were no major groups of Arabs in North Africa at all during the time period Alberto Rivera described and this did not change until the Arab conquerors captured Egypt in 639 AD. Prior to the death of Mohammed the furthest extent of the Arab permanent homelands westward was the eastern side of the Gulf of Aqaba.[69]

Saint Augustine, who Rivera claimed used his monasteries as a spy network used "to seek out and destroy Bible manuscripts owned by true Christians," was one of the great thinkers of early Christendom for Catholics, Orthodox and most main stream Protestant groups. Augustine himself was a native of North Africa who was raised by his mother as a Christian but converted to Manichaeism[70] when he was a young adult. Later Augustine did indeed adopt the religion of the Church in Rome when he and his mother, who was later to be canonized as Saint Monica, were in Milan.[71] He was teaching rhetoric at the time when he became greatly influenced by the Bishop of Milan later known as Saint Ambrose, who with Augustine,

---

[69] The Arabs in History, Bernard Lewis, Oxford University Press, 2002

[70] An ancient Persian religion originally born in the area that was Babylon. Like Zoroastrianism, it was a dualistic religion believing in the manifestation of two natures: Light (peace) and Dark (conflict).

[71] Fathers of the Church: Saint Augustine : The Trinity, Stephen McKenna, Catholic University of America Press, 1963

Gregory I and Saint Jerome, came to be known as the "Four Doctors of the West". Augustine returned to Africa after his conversion and took up the ministry. He began preaching and he founded a monastery with several other local men. His monastery was the first of a monastic system that became very important in the evangelism of North Africa during this time.[72] As prior mentioned, Augustine, later became known as "Augustine of Hippo" as he was made Bishop of Hippo Regius in 396 AD.

Augustine was very active in promoting the form of Christianity that he personally followed. The idea of the "just war"[73] had St. Augustine as one of its early formulators and he also later advocated the use of force against the heretical Donatists,[74] reasoning the Church should be able to use force against the them because the they were "lost sons" who were compelling other Christians to their

---

[72] Historical Sketches, Volume II, John Henry Cardinal Newman, Longmans, Green and Company, 1906, Chapter 9

[73] Augustine and Politics as Longing in the World, John von Heyking, University of Missouri Press, 2001

[74] The Donatists lived in the Roman Africa Province and were strong during the fourth and fifth centuries. They were a branch of Christianity founded by the Berber Christian Donatus Magnus. Donatist primary argument with the rest of the Church was regarding the treatment of those who left Christianity Persecution of Diocletian. The rest of the Church was far more forgiving of these people than the Donatists were. Donatists refused to accept spiritual authority of the religious leaders who had fallen away from the faith during the persecution, several of whom the Donatists called "traditors" (those who handed over) because these church leaders had turned in Christians for persecution and handed over Christian books and writings over to the Romans to be burned. Many church leaders had gone so far as to turn Christians over to Roman authorities and had handed over sacred religious texts to authorities to be publicly burned. These traditors had been returned to their old positions of authority under Constantine's rule, and the Donatists rebelled by declaring that any sacraments celebrated by these priests and bishops were invalid as they were not true believers.

destruction.[75] And it should be well noted that Augustine also urged the Christians to stay and fight against the invading Vandals and resist their attacks because these Germanic Vandals were part of the Arian[76] heresy.

Rather than showing Augustine as supporting the Christian Church's domination of politics, John von Heyking[77] argues that he held a subtler view of the relationship between religion and politics, one that preserves the independence of political life. And while many see his politics as based on a natural-law ethic or on one in which authority is conferred by direct revelation, von Heyking shows how Augustine held to an understanding of political ethics that emphasizes practical wisdom and judgment in a mode that resembles Aristotle rather than Machiavelli.

Alberto has gotten it all wrong about Khadijah as well.

---

[75] St. Augustine brings up this question in his "The Correction of the Donatists"

[76] Arianism was a Christological view held by followers of Arius, a fourth century Alexandria priest who taught in Egypt in the early 4th century. Arius taught that God the Father and the Son were not co-eternal, seeing the pre-incarnate Jesus as a divine being but nonetheless created by and inferior to the God the Father. They believed that Christ could not have existed prior to Jesus incarnate. Mainstream Christians of the day considered this heresy, which led to the Oriental Orthodox schism (Chaldean Church, Assyrian Church, or together commonly known as the Church of the East). For more see:
When Jesus Became God: The Struggle to Define Christianity during the Last Days of Rome, Richard E. Rubenstein, Harvest Books, 2000; and
Arius: Heresy and Tradition, Rowan Williams, Wm. B. Eerdmans Publishing Company, 2002

[77] Augustine and Politics As Longing in the World, John von Heyking, University of Missouri Press, 2001

Khadijah bint Khuwaylid was Mohammad's first wife.[78] She was approximately 15 years his senior. Khadijah had been married twice and widowed twice. After the death of her second husband she needed someone who was trustworthy who could manage her business. Mohammed was recommended by several upstanding Mecca's thus Khadijah hired him and her business continued to prosper. After approximately three years Khadijah proposed marriage to Mohammed. Khadijah became the first woman to accept Islam and she supported him in spreading the new religion. In the year 619 AD Khadijah died as did Mohammed's uncle Abu Talib. This became known to Muslims as the "Year of Sorrow" or "Year of Sadness". Khadijah was buried in Mecca.

Outside of the Quran and other subsequent Islamic writings there is no writing contemporary writing concerning Khadijah in any other language. There have been no Christian or pagan sources of the time period that tell us anything about Khadijah. And it is important to note that even though there have been monastic ruins found in the Persian Gulf area of the Arabian Peninsula, there have been no ruins of monasteries or convents in the Hejaz region where Khadijah lived and worked. Although the area around modern day Israel, Palestine, the Levant, Iraq and Syria all have several historic convents, the nearest convent this author could find discussed in any literature about the region, either religious or historical, was one devoted to

---

[78] See: The Scimitar and the Veil, Jennifer Heath, Hidden Spring Books, 2004; and Khadijah bint Khuwaylid, Dr. Daud Abdullah, Abul Qasim Publishing House (no publication date given, as such ISBN: 9960792277)

Saint Catherine[79] on the Mount of Almonds in the Sinai Peninsula in what is now modern day Egypt. This is not even on the Arabian Peninsula where Khadijah live.

It is not impossible that Khadijah might have been a Christian in that she did have Christian relatives, or at least one, her noted cousin Waraqah ibn Nawful. But we do know that she did not die a Christian, which calls to question Alberto Rivera's assertion. If Khadijah had been such a devoted follower of Christianity and was "on assignment from the Pope" to create a false religion, why would she give up Christianity for a religion she knew to be false? I can only suppose Alberto and his apologists would answer that it was all an act. But it would be an act that makes no sense at all to a rational person who was at the same time a person of a faith that tells her that she would be risking eternal damnation for such acts.

And what of "Waraqua" in Alberto Rivera's story? Who exactly was he?

Before we get into who this man was, let's get his name right. Although in his comic book tract, The Prophet, Jack Chick spelled the

---

[79] This is mentioned by the famed British explorer, soldier, translator and writer Captain Sir Richard Francis Burton (March 19, 1821 – October 20, 1890) in his book Land of the Median (Kessinger Publishing, 2004; first published in 1879). Burton was as superstar of the latter 19th century and is best-known traveling in disguise to Mecca during a hajj, translating The Arabian Nights (his original title was "The Book of the Thousand Nights and a Night") as well as the Kama Sutra. He explored the great lakes of Africa with John Hanning Speke in search of the source of the Nile. He also wrote many articles and books about varied and disparate subjects.

name "Waraqua", most scholars spell the name "Waraqah",[80] or more fully he is sited as "Waraqah ibn Nawfal".[81]

Waraqah was the cousin of Khadijah, Mohammad's first wife and by all accounts he was a pagan turned Christian monk. It is not clear whether Waraqah ever adopted Islam as he died quite soon after meeting Mohammed. He was the first recognize the signs of prophethood not long after Mohammad received his revelation.[82] During his first revelation, Mohammad was distressed at seeing the vision of an angel. Khadijah consoled Mohammed and took him to Waraqah. Waraqah told Mohammad that the angel, Gabriel (or Jabril), was the same one God had sent to Moses (Musa). Waraqah also warned Mohammad that the Mecca's would drive him out of Mecca but that he, Waraqah, would support Mohammad's cause.

Alberto Rivera tells us that Waraqah was a Roman Catholic monk, but the lack of the development of the Church in Rome at this time, coupled with the fact that most Arab Christians were Nestorians is a blow to this assertion. According to archeologist and author Peter Hellyer who specializes on the Arabian Peninsula and the Persian Gulf, "It would be unlikely, I think, that he [Waraqah] would have been Roman Catholic, since the dominant sector of the Church in Arabia was either Nestorian or Jacobite, as far as I recall, while the

---

[80] Or "Waraqa".

[81] Or "Waraqah bin Naufal" or other variations. But the final syllable in the first name is a "-qa" sound, not a "-qua" sound.

[82] Some Muslim theologians regard this as a fulfillment of Isaiah 29:11-18

Roman Catholic church, separated by this time from the Eastern Orthodox churches, of course, did not have a presence in the region."

Again, Nestorians were considered heretics by the Church in Rome as well as many of the Eastern Orthodox Churches, a fact that dates from the fifth century. Nestorianism is the Christological doctrine that Jesus existed as two persons, the man Jesus and the divine Son of God, or Logos, rather than as a unified person which is taught by most Christian churches. This belief was espoused by Nestorius[83] in the fifth century. This Nestorian view of Christ was condemned at the Council of Ephesus in 431 AD, and the conflict over this view led to the Nestorian schism, separating the Assyrian Church of the East from the Byzantine Church. One group of Nestorians now called the Chaldean Catholic Church, with their patriarchate in Baghdad, rejoined communion with the Roman Catholic Church only in the sixteenth century. The Church of the East and the Roman Catholic Church only recognized one another's theological positions at the end of the twentieth century. Chances are great that if Waraqah was a Christian he would have been considered a heretic by any follower of

---

[83] Nestorius (c.386 AD – c.451 AD) was the Patriarch of Constantinople. After a millennium-and-a-half of being known as a heretic, a book written by Nestorius near the end of his life was discovered in 1895, known as the Bazaar of Heracleides. In this book Nestorius denies the heresy and affirms Christ as the part of the Holy Trinity as well as incarnate. See:
The Bazaar of Heracleides, Nestorius, G. R. Driver (Translator), Leonard Hodgson (Translator), Wipf & Stock Publishers, 1999
Nestorius And His Place in the History of Christian Doctrine, Friedrich Loofs, Kessinger Publishing, 2004; and
Nestorius and His Teachings: A Fresh Examination of the Evidence, J. F. Bethune-Baker, Wipf & Stock Publishers, 1999

the Church in Rome at this time. The same would go for Khadijah, if in fact she ever was a Christian.

Nestorian views of Jesus Christ's godliness are much more consistent with the teachings of Islam as well. This would lead one more to believe that Waraqah was actually a Nestorian. Whether or not he was a Nestorian aside, it was till doubtful that Waraqah would have or even could have been a Roman Catholic.

Next Alberto Rivera makes an astonishing claim that teachers were sent to young Mohammed and he had intensive training in the works of St. Augustine which prepared him for his "great calling". And Rivera goes on to say that Mohammed was told that his enemies were the Jews and that the only true Christians were Roman Catholic. Mohammed was taught that others calling themselves Christians were actually "wicked impostors" and should be destroyed and that many Muslims believe this until the present day.

The only sources that we have that tell of Mohammed's life are the Quran, Islamic tradition and the Doctrina Iacobi[84] which are contemporary accounts of Mohammed's life. Both the Quran and

---

[84] Doctrina Iacobi is a Middle Eastern 7th century tract written in between 634 and 640 AD in Greek. Although it was written a few years after the death of Mohammed, the tract is still considered a contemporary account. It is a manuscript which gives possibly the earliest non-Muslim account of the origins of Islam. It presents quite a different Islamic historiography than found in traditional Islamic texts and it refers to Mohammed as a Judeo-Saracen (Jewish Arab) preacher touted as the Jewish Messiah. In one passage a learned old man refutes that Mohammed is a true prophet because "true prophets don't come with swords". The tract claims that the Jews and Saracens (Arabs) were allied against the Byzantines.

Islamic tradition state that Mohammed was illiterate and the Doctrina Iacobi is silent on the matter. Even if Mohammed could read he would have to have had knowledge of Latin to read and study the works of St. Augustine as there were no known Arabic translations in this day. Also the works of St. Augustine were known much better in Rome and North Africa at the time than anywhere else. This was mainly due to the fact that for around a century after Augustine's death the entire region around Hippo Regius was ruled by the Vandals. As mentioned before, the Vandals were Arian heretics. They greatly persecuted the non-Arian Christians in North Africa.[85] The Byzantines eventually up seeded the Vandals but ruled with a weak administration which lasted only until the Islamic invasions brought an end to their rule. The writings and teaching of St. Augustine at this time were preserved by monasteries, which had trouble growing during the Arian persecution of this time. The monasteries were in a holding pattern at very best.

So again, Rivera falls short of the truth.

---

[85] Victor of Vita : History of the Vandal Persecution, Texts by various ancient authors translated by J. W. Moorhead, Liverpool University Press, 1992

Leaving the Cocoon

'Muhammad began receiving "divine revelations" and his wife's Catholic cousin Waraquah helped interpret them. From this came the Koran. In the fifth year of Muhammad's mission, persecution came against his followers because they refused to worship the idols in the Kaaba.

'Muhammad instructed some of them to flee to Abysinnia where Negus, the Roman Catholic king accepted them because Muhammad's views on the virgin Mary were so close to Roman Catholic doctrine. These Muslims received protection from Catholic kings because of Muhammad's revelations.

'Muhammad later conquered Mecca and the Kaaba was cleared of idols. History proves that before Islam came into existence, the Sabeans in Arabia worshiped the moon-god who was married to the sun-god. They gave birth to three goddesses who were worshipped throughout the Arab world as "Daughters of Allah" An idol excavated at Hazor in Palestine in 1950's shows Allah sitting on a throne with the crescent moon on his chest.

'Muhammad claimed he had a vision from Allah and was told, "You are the messenger of Allah." This began his career as a prophet and he received many messages. By the time Muhammad died, the religion of Islam was exploding. The nomadic Arab tribes were joining forces in the name of Allah and his prophet, Muhammad.

The Prophet, by Jack T. Chick, Chick Publications, 1988

The statement that Waraqah helped interpret revelations is true but it is not 100% true. Waraqah helped with interpretations only in the very beginning and he had nothing to do with the recitations that became the Quran. It is mentioned in the Quran he died only a few days after having met Mohammed. As the only record that the world has of Waraqah is from Islamic recitations then Alberto Rivera has seemingly made a story from thin air.

Here is what one of Mohammed's widow's says about Waraqah:

> "Khadija then accompanied him [Mohammed] to her cousin Waraqa bin Naufal bin Asad bin 'Abdul 'Uzza, who, during the Pre-Islamic Period became a Christian and used to write the writing with Hebrew letters. He would write from the Gospel in Hebrew as much as Allah wished him to write. He was an old man and had lost his eyesight. Khadija said to Waraqa, "Listen to the story of your nephew, O my cousin!" Waraqa asked, "O my nephew! What have you seen?" Allah's Apostle described whatever he had seen. Waraqa said, "This is the same one who keeps the secrets (angel Gabriel) whom Allah had sent to Moses. I wish I were young and could live up to the time when your people would turn you out." Allah's Apostle asked, "Will they drive me out?" Waraqa replied in the affirmative and said, "Anyone (man) who came with something similar to what you have brought was treated with hostility; and if I should remain alive till the day when you will be turned out then I would support you strongly." But after a few days Waraqa died and the Divine Inspiration was also paused for a while."[86]

---

[86] Sahih al-Bukhari: The Translation of the Meanings, Volume 1, Book 1, Number 3: Narrated: 'Aisha, Muhammed Ibn Ismaiel Al-Bukhari, Muhammad M. Khan (Translator), Dar-us-Salam Publications, 1997

Further on Alberto Rivera says that the Mohammed instructed some of his followers to flee to Abyssinia[87] where "Negus, the Roman Catholic king" accepted them because of Mohammed's views on the Virgin Mary. There are a few reasons this is blatantly false.

The Ethiopian Orthodox Church is considered part of the Oriental Orthodox Churches.[88] They, like the Eastern churches we have been discussing, as well are Nestorian in their beliefs regarding the nature of Christ. Again, like we have seen before in this story the Ethiopian Orthodox Church does not believe in the dual nature of Christ,[89] which separated their church, as well as other Oriental Orthodox Churches, from the Roman Catholic and Eastern Orthodox Churches after the Council of Chalcedon in 451 AD.[90] King Negus did receive the Muslims, but he was in no way, shape or form a Roman Catholic, nor was he even theologically allied with the Roman Catholic Church.

Secondly, while it may be true that Negus's beliefs[91] about Jesus and Mary were much closer to Islamic beliefs than the Roman Catholic idea of the dual natures of Christ and the Catholic belief of Mother

---

[87] In those days the country was known as Aksum, and is now known as Ethiopia.
[88] Oriental Orthodox Churches: Armenian Apostolic Church, Coptic Orthodox Church, Eritrean Orthodox Tewahedo Church, Ethiopian Orthodox Church, Malankara Orthodox Church of India, and the Syriac Orthodox Church. Also known as the "Non-Chalcedonian churches".
[89] The Ethiopian Tewahedo Church: An Integrally African Church, Yesehaq, Winstock-Derek Publishers, 1997
[90] The Council of Chalcedon a Historical and Doctrinal Survey, R. V. Sellers, SPCK, 1953
[91] Muslims believe that Negus converted to Islam, but there is no historical proof to show for this.

Mary as a protector, Negus's beliefs extracted from Ethiopian orthodoxy still would have been basically inconsistent with Islam.

Then for good measure Alberto throws in the claims of the "moon god", or popularly known in the region as "Hubal",[92] which was the general Mesopotamian name for the moon god. This moon god had spread to regions in the Holy Land and in Syriac regions as well. The appearance of this statue that Rivera speaks of, which was found at Hazor,[93] in Rivera's story presents some serious problems for Rivera. First of all, the archaeologists studying the statue are undecided as to whether this statue even was a moon god. It could have represented a god, a king or a priest, and none of the experts being fully convinced one way or the other.

Here is how the statue is described...

> "The statue was found decapitated, and the head was discovered lying on a floor at a lower level. It depicts a man, possibly a priest, seated on a cube like stool. He is beardless with a shaven head; his skirt ends below his knees in an accentuated hem; his feet are bare. He holds a cup in his right hand, while his left, clenched into a fist, rests on his left knee. An inverted crescent is suspended from his necklace."[94]

---

[92] Hubal was a god worshipped in the in the lower Mesopotamia region and on the Arabian Peninsula prior to the advent of Islam.

[93] Commonly called "Hatzor" in Hebrew and "Al Hazor" in Arabic.

[94] Treasures of the Holy Land: Ancient Art from the Israel Museum, Kathleen Howard, Metropolitan Museum of Art, 1987

Most trained people who have actually studied the statue believe the statue to more likely to be a mortal human than a god due to the fact that its hands are in such a position as to appear as if it is making an offering to a deity.

Secondly, the ancient people who lived at Hazor were ancient Canaanites, not Sabeans.[95] You could not fix the name "Sabean" to them, which Alberto Rivera did. There was only one nationality in ancient times whose people were referred to as Sabeans[96] and those were the people of the legendary nation of Sheba.[97] Since the Sabeans Alberto Rivera mentioned were ostensibly from "Arabia" he could only have actually meant those people from Sheba. But these people could not have been the Sabeans of the moon god finding. Why? This was due to the fact that the Sabeans of Sheba never occupied Hazor, in the North of Israel near Galilee beyond the northern region of the Arabian Peninsula. The Sabeans were in southwestern Yemen and Ethiopia to the very far Southwest of the Arabian Peninsula and even on the African continent.

Were there any other "Sabeans" around who could rescue Alberto Rivera's story then, even if he had mistakenly named the wrong Sabeans at first?

---

[95] Also correctly known as "Sabians".
[96] Sheba: Through the Desert in Search of the Legendary Queen, Nicholas Clapp, Mariner Books, 2002
[97] Sheba, Sh'va in Hebrew and Saba in Arabic, from whence the inhabitants were called "Sabians" or "Sabeans" were in Yemen, Ethiopia or both.

There were other peoples of later times in the Middle East, many centuries later in fact, than the existence of the city of Hazor. These people were known as Sabeans and they were all around in Mohammed's day. But these Sabeans were not of any particular nationality at all.

How can that be?

The word "Sabean"[98] in its Semitic root word indicates that a person has converted from their original religion. These distinct groups of Sabeans were three separate religious minority groups, one of which was agnostic, one of which was monotheistic and one of which was polytheistic.[99]

Agnostics, as we know are non-believers in religion, not necessarily atheists, but neither believing in or conforming to any religion, thus they would not have been worshippers of Hubal.

The monotheistic Sabeans were of two kinds: non-Jews who had adopted Jewish culture and religious ideas and non-Jews (gentiles) who had adopted Christianity. Taking this into consideration, the monotheistic Sabeans would not have worshipped Hubal since Hubal was a god of a polytheistic Mesopotamian tradition. Most of the

---

[98] The Word "Sabiun" comes from the Syriac Semetic root "S-b-", referring to "conversion through submersion", which indicates that they took religions of others living in the same vicinity.
[99] The Knowledge of Life: The Origins and Early History of the Mandaeans and their Relations to the Sabians of the Qur'an and to the Harranians, Sinasi Gunduz, Oxford University Press, 1994

monotheistic Sabeans, also called Sabean Mandeans, were Gnostics and eventually moved from the Holy Land to Mesopotamia.[100] The Sabean Mandeans and the polytheist Sabeans (Yazidi) are still in existence today. And they still do not worship Hubal.

That leaves only the polytheist Sabeans, but even this does not ring true. The polytheist Sabeans[101] never in their history lived in the region of Hazor. Today they are currently inhabitants of Kurdistan in northern Iraq and Southeastern Turkey. They have been in this area since their origin in ancient times. Nevertheless, the Sabean residents of Harran now in modern day Southeast Turkey did have a moon god[102] for whom they even built a famous temple. But that god's name was not "Hubal". It was "Sin", the Akkadian version of the Sumerian "Suen".

Alberto Rivera may quite possibly have been speaking of the Nabateans, an Aramaic people who lived in the area of what is now modern day Jordan, East of Hazor running south to the Sinai Peninsula. The Nabatean capital was the world famous Petra. Even though the main Nabatean god was Dushara[103] and Nabateans also

---

[100] This may change as they have asked the current Iraqi government to provide them a safe haven homeland in Kurdistan. See: "Iraq's Minority Sabean-Mandeans seek Kurdistan Safe Haven", Agence France Press, July 5th, 2006

[101] Known to Muslims as the "Sabiuna Mushrukun", or "Pious Polytheists". And also known as "Sabeans of Harran" or even "Harranians" due to their presence in Harran, in Southeastern Turkey. They are also "Yazidi" and are centered around Mosul in Iraq.

[102] The City of the Moon God: Religious Traditions of Harran, T. M. Green, Brill Academic Publishers, 1997

[103] Petra, Maria Giulia Amadasi Guzzo, Eugenia Equini Schneider, Lydia G. Cochrane (Translator), University of Chicago Press, 2002

were known to have adopted some pre-Islamic Arab gods, even once mentioning Hubal in Nabatean writing, pinning this moon god to the Nabateans doesn't work either. The main problem with this is also the time frame again, which always seems to catch Alberto Rivera out. The Bronze Aged Hazor was destroyed by fire in the thirteenth century BC whereas the Nabateans did not even appear until nine hundred years later in the fourth century BC.

Again Alberto Rivera throws bad dice.

Arcana Imperii

'Some of Muhammad's writings were placed in the Koran, others were never published. They are now in the hands of high ranking holy men (Ayatollahs) in the Islamic faith.'

"When Cardinal Bea shared with us in the Vatican, he said, these writings are guarded because they contain information that links the Vatican to the creation of Islam. Both sides have so much information on each other, that if exposed, it could create such a scandal that it would be a disaster for both religions.

"In their "holy" book, the Koran, Christ is regarded as only a prophet. If the pope was His representative on earth, then he also must be a prophet of God. This caused the followers of Muhammad to fear and respect the pope as another "holy man."

"The pope moved quickly and issued bulls granting the Arab generals permission to invade and conquer the nations of North Africa. The Vatican helped to finance the building of these massive Islamic armies in exchange for three favors:

1. Eliminate the Jews and Christians (true believers, which they called infidels).

2. Protect the Augustinian Monks and Roman Catholics.

3. Conquer Jerusalem for "His Holiness" in the Vatican.
The Prophet, by Jack T. Chick, Chick Publications, 1988

The first question drawn from this section is regards to Mohammed's writings. As mentioned before, according to all that we know of history and Islamic tradition, Mohammed was an illiterate person. He could neither read nor write. The one and only book that is attributed to Mohammed is the Quran, which Muslims believe to have been recited to followers based on his life and his revelations from God through the angel Jabril (Gabriel). In fact, the word "Quran" in Arabic means "recitation". Some of these followers did actually write down the recitations but they were strongly recommended to memorize them. This was partially out of tradition and partially out of the fact that not many people of the day could read at all, thus a memorized rendition was more valuable to these people than a copy that had been written down.

Regarding the origin and development of the Quran, there are two schools of thought on this right now.

Islamic scholars proceed with the assumption that the Quran is a divine, uncreated text which is exactly the same today as when it was revealed to the Islamic prophet Mohammed. Secular scholars have adopted a number of other views, none of which assume divine origin. However, they differ strongly among themselves as to the "who", "when", and "how" of Quranic composition.

Mohammad could neither read nor write, but would simply recite what was revealed to him for his companions to write down and memorize. During the time revelations were received by the Prophet of Islam, the Muslims were encouraged to memorize the recitations. This is mentioned in the Hadith of Bukhari.[104] Many religious historians believe something similar to this.[105] Uthman ibn Affan,[106] the third caliph of Islam, ordered the collection of the recitations of Mohammed to be gathered together and put into a final form of the Quran, which debatably we know today. Some scholars, mainly non-Muslims, though, do not believe that Uthman collected the entire Quran nor do they believe that the Quran was collected all at one time, but that the Quran had a slow maturation process. Some of the better known historians of the Quran point to the fact that the earliest surviving copies are from later on in the ninth century and that variations of the written Quran have actually been found.

Gerd Rüdiger Puin is one such specialist.

Puin, a professor at Saarland University in Saarbrücken, Germany, is a world renowned specialist on Arabic calligraphy and Arab paleontology. Back in the early 1970's he was part of an effort to restore old quranic parchments that had been unearthed while the Great Mosque of Sana'a was being refurbished. "So many Muslims

---

[104] Al-Bukhari's Authentic Hadiths, by Muhammad Saed Abdul-Rahman (Editor), MSA Publication Ltd, 1996
[105] Introduction to the Qur'an, W. Montgomery. Watt, Edinburgh University Press, 2001
[106] The third Sunni Caliph. One of the "Four Righteously Guided Caliphs." He reigned from 644 until 656.

have this belief that everything between the two covers of the Koran is just God's unaltered word[107]," he says. "They like to quote the textual work that shows that the Bible has a history and did not fall straight out of the sky, but until now the Koran has been out of this discussion. The only way to break through this wall is to prove that the Koran has a history too…"

So Alberto Rivera's statement regarding Mohammed's "secret writings" is shown to be false in either way one looks at it.

If one accepts the Muslim belief that Mohammed was an illiterate and wrote nothing at all and that his revelations were collected by the caliph Uthman ibn Affan then the point is already moot. It would be impossible for Mohammed to have had "secret writings" if he wrote nothing.

On the other hand, if one accepts the secular approach of leading scholars that the Quran evolved over time with possibly several contributors, that the Quran was actually put down on paper sometime around the ninth century, then again Rivera would have been absolutely off the mark as Mohammed died in the seventh century.

I have shown now that there can be no such writings from Mohammed but I will take this a step further again.

---

[107] Quotes from "What is the Koran?", article by Toby Lester, The Atlantic Monthly, January, 1999

Even if such writings existed these would not have been kept closely and guarded by Ayatollahs. An Ayatollah[108] is a high rank given to major Shia clerics who have shown themselves to be very well learned and educated in the Islamic faith.[109] They are basically the ultimate religious authorities for Shias, who are a minority sect in Islam. These people run Islamic schools, or "howzehas". Although some of the Grand Ayatollahs have carried political clout and are known around the world through our news media, (such as the Ayatollah Ruhollah Khomeini, Ayatollah Ali Al-Sistani, Ayatollah Ali Khameini, and Ayatollah Mohammad Hussein Fadlullah), most of the ayatollahs are quite simply very well known religious experts in the Shia world.

Using the common sense rule again, should there be proof in writing that the Catholic Church guided the creation of a sham religion in order to use Arabs to eliminate the Roman Catholic Church's early Christian competitors, why would an ayatollah continue to worship his religion, especially if he knew from Mohammed's own writings that the religion is false? Would a man of faith who has devoted his life to the study of what his religion says is right or wrong be able to read "secret" books that would call into question the very credence of the Prophet who's words he follows, then only to turn a blind eye and continue to "closely guard" the book that would prove your faith to be mislaid

---

[108] The word "Ayatollah" means "Sign of God". Ayatollahs are all specialists in ethics, philosophy, law, mysticism and other aspects of Islamic studies.
[109] Doctrines of Shi`i Islam: A Compendium of Imami Beliefs and Practices, Ayatollah Jafar Sobhani, Reza Shah Kazemi (Translator), I. B. Tauris, 2001

It would be apostasy for either religion!

To believe this irresponsible claim to be feasible would be the equivalent of saying that Muslim leaders don't truly believe in their own religion, which is undoubtedly not the case. The only place where Alberto Rivera would be right in this part of the statement is when he says that such proof would have created a scandal.

Fortunately, the rest of his statement was also untrue.

Moving along in the text Rivera then declares that Muslims consider the pope is a "prophet of God" rationalizing that because Muslims believe Jesus to have been a prophet and the pope is his representative on earth, then the Pope himself is a prophet, or at least a de facto prophet. This is such a stretch of imagination that it belies logic.

First of all, one of the very basic and most important beliefs in Islam is that Mohammed is, was, and always will be the final prophet of God.[110] No Muslim who knows his own religion would ever consider that any person who was born after the life of Mohammed could ever possibly be a prophet. To believe such thing is heresy. To believe such a thing would automatically mean that this person is not a Muslim at all.

---

[110] And Muhammad Is His Messenger: The Veneration of the Prophet in Islamic Piety, Annemarie Schimmel, University of North Carolina Press, 1985

Secondly, there is not any tenant in Islam that mentions the pope as being Jesus Christ's representative on earth, or even God's representative anywhere and in any fashion for that matter. Although different Muslims throughout the ages may have made comments about the pope's position in the Roman Catholic Church, Islamic tradition does not get involved in recognizing hierarchical or pastoral positions within Christian denominations.

Next came the statement that the Pope "moved quickly and issued several papal bulls allowing the Arab generals to conquer North Africa". We have to look at this from several different angles.

First of all, what is a papal bull and what is its nature?

A Papal bull[111] is an open letter or declaration to Roman Catholics that is meant to issue instructions or grant privileges. It is considered a special kind of diploma, patent or charter that is written under the pope's authority. The pope's seal (bulla) is the proof of the bull's authenticity and thus this is where the name "papal bull" originates.

From the very beginning papal bulls were issued by the pope for many kinds of communications of a public nature, but after the 15th century, these bulls were only for the more solemn occasions.

---

[111] Although Papal bulls are known to have existed since the 6th century but we don't see the word until the thirteenth century, when it was only used internally. It was not an official term until the fifteenth century when the Papal chancery had created "Registrum Bullarum", or a "Register of Bulls".

There are several different kinds of papal bulls[112]. For example:

> Constitutions – These are decisions addressed to all the followers and determining some matter of faith or discipline.

> Decrees – These are affirmations or pronouncements on points affecting the general welfare of the Catholic Church.

> Decretals – Papal responses or replies to problems submitted to the Holy See, which like English common law, will carry the force of precedent.

> Encyclicals – These are letter sent either to bishops within a single country or to bishops throughout the world which are intended as outlines on how to guide their believers.

> Rescript – An apostolic letter which was sought by a prior appeal to the Pope about matters regarding the Roman Catholic Church.

All such types of papal bulls are directed to an audience of believers. These documents have absolutely no authority over non-Catholics. The first papal bull ever issued by a pope that called upon Christians to go to war[113] is known as "Quantum Praedecessores"[114] and was issued by Pope Eugene III on December 1st, 1145 AD. But even this was not a command to go to war, but a rally to Christians to go fight.

---

[112] The Catholic Encyclopedia, Volume XI, 1911 by Robert Appleton Company
[113] A History of the Crusades, vol. II: The Kingdom of Jerusalem and the Frankish East, 1100-1187, Steven Runciman, Cambridge University Press, 1952
[114] Papal bulls are rarely given titles. As such normally papal bulls are known by their first words or first sentence. This particular bull was concerning the Second Crusade after Pope Eugene III was informed by ambassadors from Jerusalem, Armenia and Antioch regarding the loss of Edessa.

The Pope offered rewards to sinners such as eternal life to sinners who died in battle. If he had commanded the Christians to go fight logic would have it that the Pope would have gone the opposite way… Spend eternity if Hell if you don't go!

Although popes commissioned and called for the Crusades, these military actions were not financed by the Catholic Church. The crusades were paid for by mainly by Catholic kings and royal benefactors as well as even the crusaders themselves.[115]

And as to the Pope financing the Arabs in their wars, assuming veracity in Alberto Rivera's fantasy that there would ever be a pope who would allow and Islamic army to go to war against Christians, one still has to ask oneself how would a pope in Rome who lived in an era when the Christian churches were still in a period of development on so many levels be able to finance huge Arab armies to attack Christians and Jews? And then after that one has to ask why five centuries later, at a time when the Roman Catholic Church was a supreme power in Europe, was the Roman Catholic Church unable to finance Christian armies to take lands back from non-Christians?

Alberto Rivera, on top of the other stretches of the imagination, goes one further and asserts that during this same time this Pope makes a *quid pro quo* with the Arab armies over the lives of Jews and Christians who were to be killed in the conquests. For papal support

---

[115] The Oxford History of the Crusades, Jonathan Riley-Smith (Editor), Oxford University Press, 2002

of the Muslims the Pope requests only two conditions: That the Augustinians and Roman Catholics are spared in the newly Arab controlled lands and that the Arab armies take the Holy Land for the Pope.

The lack of logic that Alberto Rivera used in these assertions about the popes is mind boggling to say the least. But let's offer up some of the logic for Alberto.

It is extremely likely that Muslims would not have been able to differentiate Catholics from other forms of Christianity without asking the Christians themselves, nor would they have been likely to even care about the difference. At this time, as discussed earlier in this book, there were five patriarchates in Christianity. Not all Christians looked to Rome for guidance. The majority of Christians in the world at that time looked further East to other patriarchates. And as we are constantly reminded, there were many Christian groups existing in these lands as well who were considered heretics in Rome, such as the Arians, Gnostics, Donatists and Nestorians. Almost all of these heretical Christian groups the Muslims would have felt more comfortable with because they were neighbors geographically. And the Muslims also would have found more in common with most of these groups theologically than they would have Roman Catholics. So why kill them and spare the Roman Catholics?

Muslims, when conquering much of the Middle East and North Africa, left Christianity and Judaism mainly intact as long as the Jews,

Christians and monotheistic Sabeans abided by a series of religious pacts with the Muslim rulers such as the Covenant of Umar.[116] This was neither something the Muslims decided to do on their own nor something that was requested by the Christians and Jews nor even something that the Muslims were coaxed to do from outside pressure. This was part of their Islamic religion. To remain true to the teachings of Mohammed the Children of the Book were to be left alone. Yet if Alberto Rivera was correct, the Pope would have been demanding the Muslims to deviate from their creed of protection for the Children of the Book, which the Muslims would not be able to do.

It is very important to note that prior to Umar Al-Khattab raising his army to begin the westward push across North Africa, the Arabs had already controlled Jerusalem as well as the entire Holy Land for some years prior. Also at the point of the fall of Alexandria in late 641 AD many of the Coptic Christian majority welcomed the Muslims because they had in fact been persecuted by Cyrus of Alexandria[117] (Cyrus the Melchite). So for Rivera's claim that any Pope would have been able to bargain for the Holy Land could not have been factually true in the least. Before the conquest of North Africa, the Holy Land was already firmly under Muslim rule.

---

[116] The Caliphs and their non-Muslim Subjects: a Critical Study of the Covenant of 'Umar, Arthur Stanley Tritton, Frank Cass Publisher, 1930. Christians and Jews, known in Islam as "children of the book" or "dhimmi" were allowed certain privileges and freedoms in sharia ruled states as long as they accepted Muslim rule and followed several conditions.
[117] Cyrus the Mukaukas and Melkite Patriarch of Alexandria, Anthony Alcock, Imprimerie Orientaliste, 1973

Again Alberto Rivera fails the litmus test of honesty.

The Great Backfire

"As time went by, the power of Islam became tremendous - Jews and true Christians were slaughtered, and Jerusalem fell into their hands. Roman Catholics were never attacked, nor were their shrines, during this time. But when the pope asked for Jerusalem, he was surprised at their denial! The Arab generals had such military success that they could not be intimidated by the pope - nothing could stand in the way of their own plan.

"Under Waraquah's direction, Muhammad wrote that Abraham offered Ishmael as a sacrifice. The Bible says that Isaac was the sacrifice, but Muhammad removed Isaac's name and inserted Ishmael's name. As a result of this and Muhammad's vision, the faithful Muslims built a mosque, the Dome of the Rock, in Ishmael's honor on the site of the Jewish temple that was destroyed in 70 AD. This made Jerusalem the 2nd most holy place in the Islam faith. How could they give such a sacred shrine to the pope without causing a revolt?

"The pope realized what they had created was out of control when he heard they were calling "His Holiness" an infidel. The Muslim generals were determined to conquer the world for Allah and now they turned toward Europe. Islamic ambassadors approached the pope and asked for papal bulls to give them permission to invade European countries.
The Prophet, by Jack T. Chick, Chick Publications, 1988

In a few generations Islam grew from a religion in a very remote part of the world, the Arabian Desert, to reach from the Indian Subcontinent to the Pyrenees Mountains. As we just touched on, there is a common misconception in the world that the conversion of Jews and Christians in these areas were strictly based upon "convert or die" tactics used by the new Islamic rulers. Although there were cases of this, this applied much more to polytheists than to the dhimmi, or Children of the Book (monotheists). In many parts of the conquered areas, early Christians did not see Islam as too far of a jump from their own beliefs, especially with the Christian groups that had not adopted the Nicene Creed. Another big factor was that the Byzantine Empire was very corrupted in the Middle East and North Africa and many Christians welcomed the change of rule to the Muslim invaders.

This is explained well again by Dr. Farouq Dawood.:

"There are historical documents that the Patriarchs, the heads of this Church in Iraq in Seleucia-Ctesiphon[118] did not object to the spread of Islam; on the contrary, there was sympathy. There was no confrontation between the Christians of Mesopotamia in general, and in Iraq in particular, and the Muslims. Also, there were at the time Christians who were Arabs like those of Hira, the Al-Manathera, as well as Al-Ghassanis who were Arab groups. Also, there were other Arab tribes that were Christian, like Bani-Taglob and Bani-Tay and others. Those entered Islam very easily because it was their civilization and their language.

---

[118] Seleucia-Ctesiphon is one of the great cities of ancient Mesopotamia. It was known under many names over the years and had been the capital of the Parthian Sassanid Empires. It is believed by many that Ctesiphon was the largest city in the world from 570 to 637. The Greek colony of Seleucia was a twin city across the Tigris River, thus the two cities together were often known by a common hyphenated name Seleucia-Ctesiphon. This city pre-dated Baghdad and its ruins are within 30 km of Baghdad.

However, most of the Christians kept their religion. Those that entered Islam were the Zoroastrians, or other idol worshipping religions. Why? Because, Islam did not force the Christians to become Muslims, but only to pay "Jezya".[119] They were considered people of the book. Many years later, you find not only peaceful living but shared living conditions between Christians and Muslims. The proof to that is there were religious dialogues at the highest level, for example, the dialogue between the Patriarch Timthaowes the Great, around 800 AD with the Khalifa Al-Mahdi. Also, the dialogue of Bishop Eliya Bershinaya, Bishop of Nissibin with the minister Al-Maghrebi...

"[These were] dialogues between Christians and Muslims about God, about miracles, about salvation and about punishment, etc. Add to that there were dialogues between scientists and philosophers between Christians and Muslims. For example, in Baghdad, the capital of the Abassid Khalifate, especially, at Al-Zaera and Al-Majeda, the schools were mixed, i.e., there was no discrimination between Christians and Muslims, especially in science schools and philosophy, in science of logic. The head of 'House of Wisdom' was a Christian, but had Muslims working in it, or was run by a Sabean and had Christians and Muslims working in it or was run by a Muslim and vice-versa. Same in hospitals like 'Al-Radi' we see working in Father Ibin Al-Tayab."[120]

Further to the above, where we see that the children of the book were not always "put to the sword" as is a common misconception that

---

[119] Jezya was a tax required to be paid from dhimmi, the children of the book. In other words, Jews and Christians could keep their heritage and religion under certain circumstances. Jezya was one.

[120] Again from "Chaldeans of Iraq: Past and Present", Interview of Fr. Yousif Habbi, Al Jazeera, Broadcasted on November 5th, 2000. Yousif Habbi was the pen name Dr. Farouq Dawood used.

Alberto Rivera played on, there is also absolutely no proof in history that any pontiff ever asked for the Holy Land after it had been conquered by the Arabs. It also doesn't mean that Christians weren't killed during this time. It was, after all, a time of war.

Prior to the First Crusade, on November 27th, 1095 AD, Pope Urban II at the Council of Claremont declared that a war to bring back the Holy Land to Christian rule was a *bellum sacrum*.[121] But this was not aimed at a Muslim audience. It was for the ears of 300 clerics from throughout France, as well as many powerful Christian lords who the Pope asked the clerics to bring along.[122] It was here that the Pope asked these clerics and lords to basically take the riff raff of their lands and send them to fight for what was more than a just cause, getting a second lease on life with the promise that anyone dying in this cause would go to heaven. These words from Urban II never fell on Muslim ears.

Rivera then claims that Waraqah instructed Mohammed what to put into the Quran, but from what we have already been over in this book, we can reject this statement right out of hand. We have already discussed the fact that Mohammed could not read nor write and that he did not write the Quran, nor could he have as the Quran was not even written down in his life time. We also have established that Waraqah died not long after meeting Mohammed so even if he could

---

[121] Latin for "holy war", which is a higher level of conflict than a "bellum iustum", or "just war".
[122] The Speech of Pope Urban II at Clermont, 1095, Dana Carleton Munro, Macmillan, 1906

have told Mohammed what needed to be in the Quran, he would have
been quite unable to do so when he was dead. But the rest of Rivera's
above statement concerning the difference between the Judeo-
Christian position on Isaac and Ishmael vs. the Muslim position on
the same brothers, (Ishaq and Ismail), is basically true. And Muslims
do believe the area where the Dome of the Rock is built to be the
place where Ismail (Ishmael) was almost sacrificed to Allah and
Christians and Jews believe this was the site where Isaac (Ishaq) was
almost sacrificed.

But Alberto Rivera makes some more mistakes here.

The Dome of the Rock, built on this site from 687 AD to 691 AD by
Abd Al-Malik, the ninth Caliph, even though it is sometimes referred
to as a mosque, [123] in reality it is not a mosque at all. It is only a
sanctuary. And like we have shown previously in this book, the site is
not the second holiest place in Islam per Rivera's testimony.
Together with Al-Aqsa Mosque, which is adjacent to the structure, it
is the third holiest place in Islam[124] after Al-Kaaba in Mecca and
Masjid Al-Nabawi, or "Mosque of the Prophet", which is in Medina.

As we will see in the next chapter, the Moorish conquest of the
Iberian Peninsula began approximately twenty years after the Dome
of the Rock was fully complete but this conquest took place over 380

---

[123] It is sometimes referred to though as the "Mosque of Umar" because it is the site
where Umar prayed upon capturing Jerusalem.
[124] The Dome of the Rock, Said Nuseibeh, Rizzoli, 1996

years before the First Crusade. There is no record that the Berbers[125] and Umayyad Arabs[126] who took the Iberian Peninsula consulted anyone but their own hierarchy in this effort[127] or that they sent any ambassadors to Rome to ask the Pope to issue any bulls on the matter. And as pointed out previously, papal bulls that are issued in reply to situational issues[128] are only issued regarding church matters, not temporal matters, thus a papal bull could not even have been requested.

Another point that Alberto Rivera forgot when he was making his statement about the Arab conquests in Europe is that the Visigoths ruled the Iberian Peninsula region, thus this part of Europe was outside of the Roman Catholic Church. (Remember, the Visigoths were Arian heretics…). In either case there would have been no reason to consult with anyone from Christendom prior to conquest.

For a Spaniard claiming to have been a Jesuit priest at one time, I would have thought Alberto Rivera would have known very well that piece of history about his former religion and his nation of birth.

---

[125] The general who lead the conquest was not an Arab but actually a Berber who's name was Tariq ibn Ziyad. Gibraltar is named for his landing. The name is a Spanish corruption of the Arabic words "Jebel Al-Tariq", or "Tariq's mountain".
[126] The Umayyads were the first dynasty of Arab caliphs after the death of Mohammad. They ultimately ruled the Arab world mainly from Damascus.
[127] The Moors: The Islamic West 7th-15th Centuries AD, David Nicolle, Osprey Publishing, 2001
[128] Decretals and Rescripts.

The Crusades

"The Vatican was outraged; war was inevitable. Temporal power and control of the world was considered the basic right of the pope. He wouldn't think of sharing it with those whom he considered heathens.

"The pope raised up his armies and called them crusades to hold back the children of Ishmael from grabbing Catholic Europe. The crusades lasted centuries and Jerusalem slipped out of the pope's hands. "
The Prophet, by Jack T. Chick, Chick Publications, 1988

Before I get into the First Crusade I would like to discuss the term "temporal power" that Alberto Rivera is ascribing to the Pope at this time. What exactly kind of power is "temporal power"? By definition, in this sense which we are referring, "temporal" is:

> "Of or relating to the material world; worldly: the temporal possessions of the Church."[129]

Thus, papal temporal power is the political and ruling activity of the papacy, separately from their "eternal power".[130] The popes first had the use of temporal power bestowed upon them in a *de facto* way during the Byzantine era when the Byzantines were forced to retreat from parts of the Italian Peninsula.

---

[129] The American Heritage® Dictionary of the English Language: Fourth Edition. 2000

[130] Power relating to spiritual, missionary, and ministry authority.

What lead up to this?

As we know, the Christian religion spent its first three centuries in the Roman Empire as an untolerated and even outlawed religion. Thus any Christian organization, such as the Church that was based in Rome which eventually developed into the Roman Catholic Church, could not legally hold property, transfer property or even collect money from its believers. When Constantine I made all religions within the empire legal the Church in Rome very quickly grew in wealth and stature[131] and this was boosted yet again when Christianity was made the state religion several decades later. During this time the Church held these properties as a private property holder, not as a sovereign. In the fifth century though, during a power vacuum between the demise of the Western Roman Empire under Rome's last emperor Romulus Augustus[132] and the rule of Odoacer's Kingdom of Italy falling to Theodoric the Great and his Ostrogoths, the Church began to assume sovereign authority based upon the assertion of spiritual supremacy.

The ultimate use of temporal power, the papacy with its own nation, began in the sixth century[133] and lasted until 1870 in the form of the

---

[131] Early on Constantine I gave the first significant donation of property, the Lateran Palace.

[132] The Fall of the Roman Empire: A New History of Rome and the Barbarians, Peter Heather, Oxford University Press, 2005

[133] The Republic of St. Peter: The Birth of the Papal State, 680-825, Thomas F. X. Noble, University of Pennsylvania Press, 1986

Papal States[134] and re-continued with the Lateran Treaties in 1929 as the Vatican City.

Having discussed the Pope's temporal powers and "control of the world", as so nominated by Alberto Rivera, it is interesting to note that Rivera disregards the fact that the Pope's temporal powers stopped at the borders of the Papal States. His "control of the world" was only the control within the Papal States, which was loose at best. Yes, the Pope could exercise certain political powers abroad[135], especially through his spiritual authority, but this is not a direct power he wields, it is in reality very indirect.

A good example of what is meant when we say that the Pope relies on world leaders for his powers can be seen when we look at the nation that was run by popes for centuries. The Papal States themselves were originally outlined by Charlemagne, not the Pope. The beginning, existence and independence of the Papal States were dependent upon treaties, alliances and mutual recognitions of other nations for the very survival of the Papal States, not resting on papal authority. By no means did the Pope's secular temporal power ever extend to the control of the world and it could not be seen as the basic right of the Pope if such treaties were required. A point making this very clear is that when the papacy first began to assert temporal

---

[134] The end of the Papal States coincides with the emergence of the Italian nation. Although the Vatican considered that their temporal authority did not end during this time and thus the popes, after the capture of Rome by Italian nationalists, considered themselves as "prisoner of Italy".

[135] The Line of Demarcation, dividing the world between Spanish and Portuguese spheres of influence is a good example of this.

power, every citizen in the area later known as the Papal States, including the Pope himself, were still *de jure* citizens of the Byzantine Empire.[136] This didn't change until the days of Charlemagne.

On to the Crusades...

The causes of the beginning of the Crusades[137] had nothing to do with the Muslims, led by Umar ibn Al-Khattab, capturing Jerusalem and the Holy Land as Alberto Rivera so claims.

There is a very simple fact that makes this clear.

The Arabs conquered Jerusalem in 638 AD, a full 457 years before Pope Urban II spoke out in favor of the "just war" and a full 461 years before fighting from the First Crusade even reached Jerusalem.

Although the first crusades were Roman Catholic holy wars that eventually aimed to recapture Jerusalem and the Holy Land from the Islamic rulers, it should be well noted that not all of the Crusades were even fought against Muslims.[138] A good example is the Albigensian Crusade against the Cathars, Christian Gnostic heretics of southern France. There were also the Northern Crusades which were directed at the peoples living in Central and Northern Europe (pagan

---

[136] Byzantium: Empire of the New Rome, Cyril Mango, Phoenix, 2005
[137] The Crusades were a series of military campaigns, some led by knights and royalty, others by peasants and lay people, that were fought during the 11th through 13th centuries. Most of these were sanctioned by the Pope.
[138] The First Crusade: A New History: The Roots of Conflict between Christianity and Islam, Thomas Asbridge, Oxford University Press, 2005

Baltic peoples, Finns, Prussians and Orthodox Russians). And then there was the Fourth Crusade which conquered Constantinople and weakened it even more against its Muslim adversaries.

How the Crusades all started...

In 1095 AD the Byzantine Emperor Alexius I[139] requested 500 Flemish knights from the Pope at the Council of Piacenza. He did this through Ambassadors from other states. Alexius needed the Flemish knights in order to defend his empire against the Muslim Seljuk Turks. In 1095 AD at the Council of Clermont Pope Urban II spoke out and called upon all Christians to participate in a war against the Turks, a religious war which would count as full penance for its participants. The cause and purpose of the war was not originally the capture Jerusalem.

Crusader armies in the First Crusade came in two waves. The first group, led by Peter the Hermit[140], was annihilated while still in Asia Minor. In 1099 AD the second wave of crusaders succeeded in taking Jerusalem after sacking many cities in their path. Once in Jerusalem

---

[139] Alexios I Komnenos in Greek or Alexius I Comnenus in Latin (1048–August 15, 1118), Byzantine emperor (1081 AD – 1118 AD), was the first emperor of the Komnenian restoration of the Byzantine Empire, and the founder of the Komnenian army.

[140] Peter the Hermit (? -1131 AD) was a recluse priest of Amiens, France, and important player during the First Crusade. Peter preached and recruited in France for the Crusade and led the first wave. Prior to the Crusade Peter the Hermit had once been a pilgrim to the Holy Land but was stopped by the Turks and tortured and thus failed to complete the journey.

they massacred much of the population, including Christians, Muslims and Jews in the process.

Prior to the crusades, as early as 1090 AD, Alexius I had taken a few reconciliatory measures towards the Papacy. He had the intention of seeking future western support against the Seljuks in order to protect his own empire. When in 1095 AD his ambassadors appeared before Pope Urban II at the Council of Piacenza, they reported that the help which Alexius wanted from the West was simply a small mercenary force, the Flemish knights. This particular request was made possibly in order to establish a precedent. But Alexius did not expect the immense hosts which arrived, to his great consternation and personal embarrassment. Not quite ready to supply this number of people as they traversed across Byzantine territories, the emperor saw his Balkan possessions subjected to further pillage at the hands of his own Christian allies. Alexius I dealt with the first disorganized riff raff group of crusaders, led by the preacher Peter the Hermit, by pushing them on to Asia Minor, where they were massacred by the Turks in 1096 AD.

A second and much stronger and better organized wave of crusaders[141] later made its way to Constantinople. As this wave arrived in Byzantium in two separate groups thus Alexius used the opportunity of consulting with leaders separately. He was able to get from the leaders the promise to turn over conquered lands to

---

[141] Led by Raymond IV of Toulouse, Godfrey of Bouillon, and Bohemund of Taranto.

Constantinople as well as homage from the leaders upon Alexius's agreement to supply the crusaders with provisions. The Byzantine Empire was able thusly to recapture many islands and cities that were previously lost. But the Byzantines failed to help with the siege of Antioch. As such the Crusaders considered they had been double crossed and deemed then that their oaths of homage were hence voided. This led to strained relations and repercussions on both sides down the road.

The First Crusade was the most successful against the Muslims as several Christian kingdoms were founded, but these were only to be lost to the Muslims again prior to the Second Crusade.[142]

As we have seen by looking at history we know that Pope Urban II didn't start the Crusades per se, as claimed by Alberto Rivera, but was asked by the Byzantine Emperor for help. And although the Crusades did cover a time period of about two centuries, we have shown that many of these crusades simply had nothing to do with fighting Muslims.

Alberto claims that the Pope was preventing the Muslims from capturing "Catholic Europe". While this may have been one of the considerations of the Pope at the time, the reality was that the that the Great Schism between the Roman Catholic Church and the Eastern Orthodox churches had already occurred around four decades

---

[142] The New Concise History of the Crusades, Updated Edition, Thomas F. Madden, Rowman & Littlefield Publishers Inc., 2005

earlier,[143] so the protection offered by the fighting crusaders of the First Crusade was more realistically for orthodox Christians, not Roman Catholics. Of course one aim that came out of this all was to retake of the Holy Land for Christians, and like we saw, this was nominally successful for a while.

---

[143] A History of the Papacy from the Great Schism to the Sack of Rome, Mandell Creighton, Kessinger Publishing, 2005

Détente

"Turkey fell and Spain and Portugal were invaded by Islamic forces. In Portugal, they called a mountain village 'Fatima' in honor of Muhammad's daughter, never dreaming it would become world famous.

"Years later when the Muslim armies were poised on the islands of Sardinia and Corsica, to invade Italy, there was a serious problem. The Islamic generals realized they were too far extended. It was time for peace talks. One of the negotiators was Francis of Assisi.

"As a result, the Muslims were allowed to occupy Turkey in a 'Christian' world, and the Catholics were allowed to occupy Lebanon in the Arab world. It was also agreed that the Muslims could build mosques in Catholic countries without interference as long as Roman Catholicism could flourish Arab countries.

"Cardinal Bea told us in Vatican briefings that both the Muslims and Roman Catholics agreed to block and destroy the efforts of their common enemy, Bible-believing Christian missionaries. Through these concordats, Satan blocked the children of Ishmael from a knowledge of Scripture and the truth.

"A light control was kept on Muslims from the Ayatollah down through the Islamic priests, nuns and monks. The Vatican also engineers a campaign of hatred between the Muslim Arabs and the Jews. Before this, they had co-existed peacefully.

"The Islamic community looks on the Bible-believing missionary as a devil who brings poison to the children of Allah. This explains years of ministry in those countries with little results."
The Prophet, by Jack T. Chick, Chick Publications, 1988

Again Rivera panders to those who aren't familiar with history.

Virtually all of the eastern region and much of the central region of the Turkey's Anatolian Peninsula, also called Asia Minor, which is the land mass that makes up the Asian majority of Turkey today, was controlled by the Seljuk Turks at the time of the First Crusade. The Byzantine Empire controlled the far West of Asia Minor and most of the coastal areas. Alberto Rivera ignores the fact that at the end of the crusades this was still the case. "Turkey", as Alberto Rivera called this area using its modern day name, had not yet fallen. Constantinople, the modern day Istanbul, stood until 1453 AD.[144] The vast majority of Spain and Portugal on the other hand were lost during the Moorish invasions, between 711 – 718 AD[145] over 300 years before the First Crusade and well over 700 years before the fall of Constantinople.

Another falsehood was that the Moors in Iberia named the Portuguese town Fátima after Fatima Zahra, Mohammed's daughter. This will be explained in much greater detail in the next chapter.

---

[144] Osman's Dream: The History of the Ottoman Empire, Caroline Finkel, Basic Books, 2006
[145] The Story of the Moors in Spain, Stanley Lane-Poole, Black Classic Press, 1990

Alberto Rivera was wrong also about Sardinia and Corsica. These two strategic islands, along with Sicily, were empty of Moorish rulers well before the crusades even began.

From their Iberian strong points the Moors began raiding Byzantine Sardinia in the eighth century, after having taken Sicily from the Byzantines. The Moors took Corsica and ruled from 850 to 1034 AD. By the year of 1090 AD no Moorish rule remained in any of the three Mediterranean islands,[146] let alone having Arabs perched and aiming a dagger at Rome's heart at the end of the crusades, per Rivera's outrageous version of history.

We also should note that Saint Francis of Assisi was born in the year 1182 AD,[147] as such, even if the Moors had been ready to attack in 1090 AD, the last year of the Moors in Sicily, giving Alberto Rivera the benefit of the doubt, there is absolutely no way Saint Francis of Assisi could have been a negotiator. He was not even born for another 92 years!

Due to the dates being so inaccurate above, we have ruled out the part of Alberto Rivera's story that any such agreement that might have happened directly between the Pope and Arab armies at the end of the

---

[146] See: Rambles in the Islands of Corsica and Sardinia: With Notices of Their History, Antiquities, and Present Condition, Thomas Forester, Adamant Media Corporation, 2004; and
History of Sicily, 800-1713: Medieval Sicily, Denis Mack Smith, Dorset Press, 1989
[147] St. Francis of Assisi: A Biography, Omer Englebert, Servant Ministries, 1979

crusades. But even so, the other *quid pro quo* that Alberto Rivera alleges concerning the Pope agreeing to allow the Muslims to "occupy Turkey" in the "Christian world" and the Catholics were allowed to "occupy Lebanon" in the "Arab world" is also factually untrue.

Again, the Seljuk Turks already were in over half of the landmass that made up modern day Turkey. After the Seljuk Turks ceased to exist as a nation the Turkic tribes in Anatolia were small emirate type entities. Later the Ottomans, one of these entities, grew in power and took all of the formerly Seljuk controlled lands plus some, eventually defeating and dealing the death blow to the Byzantine Empire. Lebanon on the other had been invaded by crusaders from 1109 AD until 1124 AD and several small independent Christian kingdoms existed temporarily, which eventually ended with the fall of Acre to the Muslims in 1291 AD.[148]

Neither of these "occupations" was by any agreement with any pope.

Also, further to the claim of concordats between the Roman Catholic Church and the Muslims to "block and destroy the efforts of their common enemy, Bible believing Christian missionaries" there are a few reasons this could not have happened.:

---

[148] A History of the Crusades: Volume 3, The Kingdom of Acre and the Later Crusades, Steven Runciman, Cambridge University Press, 1954

As pointed out prior, there were certain rights generally granted through pacts between the Christian and Jewish communities in Muslim conquered areas, such as the Covenant of Umar, but none of these would allow for evangelizing and converting new members to their faith. It was against Islam. As such, there was no need to make such an agreement with the Roman Catholic Church.

Secondly, by definition the purpose of a concordat is to "terminate, or to avert, dissension between the Church and the civil powers",[149] generally the civil powers within a Christian country that recognizes the authority of the Church. Muslims recognize the faithful, but don't recognize any authority of the Roman Catholic Church in a Muslim country, therefore there could never exist a concordat between the Roman Catholic Church and any Islamic entity, unless that entity was an Islamic republic with civil authorities, such as that of present day Iran. But should this have been the case there would have been an official record of the concordat both in the Church's possession and in the Islamic government's possession. Also, the authority of such an agreement would have existed only within the boundaries of that specific Islamic nation and would have a maximum life span only as long as the governmental structure of that Islamic nation existed.

But going back to the time period in question, even if a Muslim nation would have accepted the authority of the Roman Catholic Church and dealt directly with the Pope, at what point would a concordat have been sought and with whom? During the crusades against the Muslims the crusaders fought Muslim Turks on Asia Minor and

---

[149] The Catholic Encyclopedia, Volume XI, 1911 by Robert Appleton Company

Muslim Arabs in the Holy Land. These ruling parties also changed with the time.

Alberto Rivera next says that the Vatican kept a "light control" on the Muslims from "the Ayatollah down through the Islamic priests, nuns and monks." Without saying how he proposed it was that the Vatican could keep such a "light control" on millions of Muslims in a vast, disparate geography, many different cultures, who continued from those times to expand their presence, especially eastward, I have no idea how Alberto Rivera would even begin to back up this statement.

Alberto Rivera becomes a bit laughable when he mentions "Islamic priests, nuns and monks". There are no such positions in Islam. You do have religious men who are educated and able to lead other Muslims by word and by example. These are imams.[150]

And the claim that the Vatican "engineers a campaign of hatred between Muslim Arabs and Jews" does not hold water. Without the issue of the Israeli-Palestinian state, there would be no real conflict between Muslims and Jews. But as the situation has it, both Muslims and Jews believe that Jerusalem should be theirs and that their holy sites should not be corrupted. Jews, including Zionists who have immigrated to the Holy Land are the same. Prize-winning Israeli novelist A.B. Yehoshua recently spelled this out strongly to the community of American Jews. "For me there is no alternative," said

---

[150] In fact the word "imam" actually means "leader" in Arabic.

Yehoshua, "I cannot keep my identity outside Israel. Israel is my skin, not my jacket." [151]

The Arabs have a very similar stand. Ali Safuri, who has fought against the Israelis for a number of years as a member of Islamic Jihad, sums up the Arab position on the matter. "I have cousins in Beirut, in Syria, in Saudi Arabia, in all the countries of the world," said Safuri, "It is their right to return to their country and homeland. The son of Haifa has the right to return to his town. The person who comes from America or Russia has the right to live in Haifa and Tel Aviv, and the true son of Haifa and Tel Aviv remains homeless and exiled." [152]

This situation is not the doing of the Vatican.

Finally, apostasy is an offense in Islam that is punishable by death. Muslims do not make any distinction between Catholic priests or missionaries from any other denomination when it comes to the prosetlizing of Muslim populations. As recent headlines have been noted, even Catholic priests are targeted when Muslims see them as trying to convert Muslims. [153] This flies in the face of the Alberto

---

[151] "Jewish Tribalism Comes Clean", by Jonathan Cook, Dissident Voice Newsletter, July 1st, 2006

[152] "Battle for the Holy Land", Frontline, Interviewed by Stuart Tanner on March 27th, 2002. Aired on the Public Broadcasting System (PBS). At that time Ali Safuri was the head of the Islamic Jihad in Jenin.

[153] Some recent headlines have been "Catholic Priest Knifed in Turkey", BBC, July 2nd, 2006, and "Nigerian Priest: Another Victim of Violence Protests Exploiting Religion", L'Osservatore Romano, February 21st, 2006; and "Muslim cleric arrested for the murder of a young Catholic" by Qaiser Felix, AsiaNews, January 23rd,

Rivera's notion that the Catholics and Muslims had an understanding to persecute non-Catholic Christian missionaries in Muslim lands. Islam does not appreciate any missionaries from any religion or creed.

2006; and "Martyred: Muslim Murder and Mayhem Against Christians", by Kate O'Beirne, National Review, Dec 3, 2001

Fátima and the End Game

"The next plan was to control Islam. In 1910, Portugal was going Socialistic. Red flags were appearing and the Catholic Church was facing a major problem. Increasing numbers were against the church.

"The Jesuits wanted Russia involved, and the location of this vision at Fatima could play a key part in pulling Islam to the Mother Church.

"In 1917, the Virgin appeared in Fatima." "The Mother of God" was a smashing success, playing to overflow crowds. As a result, the Socialists of Portugal suffered a major defeat.

"Roman Catholics world-wide began praying for the conversion of Russia and the Jesuits invented the Novenas to Fatima which they could perform throughout North Africa, spreading good public relations to the Muslim world. The Arabs thought they were honoring the daughter of Muhammad, which is what the Jesuits wanted them to believe.

"As a result of the vision of Fatima, Pope Pius XII ordered his Nazi army to crush Russia and the Orthodox religion and make Russia Roman Catholic." A few years after he lost World War II, Pope Pius XII startled the world with his phoney dancing sun vision to keep Fatima in the news. It was great religious show biz and the world swallowed it.

"Not surprisingly, Pope Pius was the only one to see this vision. As a result, a group of followers has grown into a Blue Army world-wide, totaling millions of faithful Roman Catholics ready to die for the blessed virgin.

"But we haven't seen anything yet. The Jesuits have their Virgin Mary scheduled to appear four or five times in China, Russia, and major appearance in the U.S.

"What has this got to do with Islam? Note Bishop Sheen's statement: 'Our Lady's appearances at Fatima marked the turning point in the history of the world's 350 million Muslims. After the death of his daughter, Muhammad wrote that she 'is the most holy of all women in Paradise, next to Mary.'

"'He believed that the Virgin Mary chose to be known as Our Lady of Fatima as a sign and a pledge that the Muslims who believe in Christ's virgin birth, will come to believe in His divinity.'

"Bishop Sheen pointed out that the pilgrim virgin statues of Our Lady of Fatima were enthusiastically received by Muslims in Africa, India, and elsewhere, and that many Muslims are now coming into the Roman Catholic Church."

The Prophet, by Jack T. Chick, Chick Publications, 1988

In 1910 Portugal was not going "Socialistic" as Rivera so claims, or at least not in a sense that the country would have been lost to communism as Russia was years later. This was a watershed year for the Portuguese. It was the end of their constitutional monarchy, which resulted from Portugal's October 5th Revolution of that same year. The revolution was not instituted by socialists, but by nationalist republicans.

The overthrow of the constitutional monarchy created the First Republic[154] which was run initially by a group called the Portuguese Republican Party,[155] which over the course of the sixteen year life of the Republic, splintered into several smaller parties covering the entire political spectrum. The First Republic lessened the power of the president and created a weak parliamentary government that collapsed over forty times from 1910 to 1926, when a military dictatorship took over, lasting until 1974. There was no permanent broad Socialist defeat of that year as Rivera claimed, especially since the Portuguese governments of the period changed approximately every 21 weeks on average over the 16 years of the First Republic.

At this juncture[156] Alberto Rivera, or Jack Chick, makes a statement that the Jesuits wanted Russia involved in the vision of Fátima. This is most likely a reference to later visions seen by one of the three children witnesses, Lúcia Santos, who claimed to see the visions of Fátima in 1917 near the central Portugal town bearing the same name. Later in life Lúcia Santos, then a nun, in 1941 wrote down the first two of the three secrets given the children by Mary.[157] In this secret Mary said she wanted the Consecration of Russia to the Immaculate Heart[158] in order to achieve world peace. But this information is unknown from reading the comic book because this isn't specifically

---

[154] "Primeira República" in Portuguese.
[155] The Social Origins of Democratic Collapse: The First Portuguese Republic in the Global Economy, Kathleen C. Schwartzman, University Press of Kansas, 1989
[156] "The Prophet", by Jack T. Chick, Chick Publications, 1988. p. 25
[157] Lúcia did this to help with the other two children's' beatification process. These two children were her cousins and they died in the Spanish flu epidemic of 1919 and 1920.
[158] The Immaculate Heart, John de Marchi, Farrar, Straus and Young, 1952

mentioned. This is also problematic to Rivera's story due to the fact that as just pointed out this Consecration of Russia was only revealed in 1941, nearly a quarter century after the incident, not in 1917. And although it is undoubtable that some devout Catholics began to pray for the Consecration of Russia right away after this second secret of Our Lady of Fátima was revealed, still the time frame does not fit with Alberto Rivera's story by twenty-four years.

There was in fact a novena[159] written to honor Our Lady of Fátima and according to Catholic sources[160] there have been some Muslims pilgrimages to Fátima but it is unlikely that saying novenas throughout North Africa would be "spreading good public relations to the Muslim world" per Alberto Rivera's testimony. A few reasons for this:

1) Novenas are normally said alone, in private, and heard only by the person saying the novena.
2) It is a Roman Catholic personal ceremony, and Muslims would not be partaking of this.

The tract refers to the fact that Arabs thought the Jesuits were honoring the daughter of Mohammad by creating these novenas. Again, Muslims would be very, very unlikely to ever hear a Catholic reciting novenas, but at the same time it must be made clear that the

---

[159] A novena is one of the sacramentals of the Roman Catholic Church. It is a devotional prayer that is said over nine successive days which request special graces or privileges.
[160] "Our Lady and Islam: Heaven's Peace Plan", by Father Ladis J. Cizik, Soul Magazine, September - October, 2001

town of Fátima was also not named after Mohammad's daughter as Alberto Rivera so clearly stated. Not directly anyway.

The name of the Portuguese town actually comes from the Arabic word "Fatima",[161] and yes, Mohammed's beloved daughter's name was Fatima Zahra. And yes, Fatima has been a popular name for Muslim women for centuries in great part because of Fatima's high esteem with followers of Islam worldwide. But according to José Saramago[162] the name of the town Fátima comes from an Iberian Muslim princess, most likely the daughter of an Arab ruler, who was captured by Christian forces during the Moorish occupation of Portugal. This Fátima was forced into marriage to the Count of Ourém. In 1158 AD, prior to the marriage she was converted to Catholicism, with the baptismal name Oureana, as the Count's dominion, Ourém, derived its name from the name "Oureana".[163] Oureana's old Arabic name, Fátima, was given to the parish within this municipality, which carries her name to this day.[164]

Given that the origin of the village name "Fátima" is not from Fatima Zahra but rather from an Arab princess who apostated and converted to Christianity, it is extremely highly unlikely that neither Arab Muslims nor any other Muslims for that matter, would be very honorific toward this Christian Holy site.

---

[161] In Arabic meaning "one who weans".
[162] José Saramago is a journalist and author who won the Nobel Prize for Literature in 1998.
[163] Oriana in English.
[164] Journey to Portugal: In Pursuit of Portugal's History and Culture, José Saramago, Amanda Hopkinson (Translator), Nick Caistor (Translator), Harvest Books, 2002

Turning to the Second World War, Alberto Rivera recklessly claims that Pope Pius XII held the reigns over the Nazi war machine. This is an extremely irresponsible position. It is true that Pius, a staunchly anti-communist pope, initially felt that the Germans were a buffer between the communist Soviet Union and mainly Catholic Western Europe. And while there have been revisionist histories written that have been very critical of Pius XII for not raising his voice against Nazi Germany or even claiming that the Roman Catholic Church through financial dealings or helping suspected criminals to relocate out of Europe[165] indirectly helped the Nazi cause, there also have been many verifiable accounts regarding Pius's involvement in saving hundreds of thousands of Jews.[166]

One of the plainest rebuttals to claims of Pope Pius XII's silence regarding the Nazis is issued by famed Italian historian, Antonio Spinosa, who has written nearly half a dozen books about the leaders on both sides of the second world war.:

---

[165] See: Unholy Trinity: The Vatican, The Nazis, & The Swiss Banks, Mark Aarons, John Loftus, St. Martin's Griffin, 1998; and
Hitler's Pope: The Secret History of Pius XII, John Cornwell, Penguin, 2000; and
The Catholic Church and Nazi Germany, Guenter Lewy, Da Capo Press, 2000; and
The Catholic Church and the Holocaust, 1930-1965, Michael Phayer, Indiana University Press, 2001

[166] See: Righteous Gentiles: How Pius XII and the Catholic Church Saved Half a Million Jews from the Nazis, Ronald J. Rychlak, Spence Publishing Company, 2005; and
The Myth of Hitler's Pope: How Pope Pius XII Rescued Jews from the Nazis, David G. Dalin, Regnery Publishing, 2005; and
Pope Pius XII: Architect for Peace, Margherita Marchione, Paulist Press, 2000; and
Pius XII and the Second World War: According to the Archives of the Vatican, Pierre Blet, Lawerence J. Johnson (Translator), Paulist Press, 1999

"To continue accusing Pius XII of having fallen silent before the persecutions,' continued Spinosa, 'is an action in bad faith, because it does not consider the reasons for the silence, an apparent silence because the Pope tried to avoid that his words would provoke a more vicious reaction from Hitler. It was a silence that accompanied a powerful action in defense of the Jews: he opened the very doors of the Vatican to them in order to save the greatest number possible. This happened not only in Rome, but also in other parts of Europe, to the point that at least 800,000 Jews owe their lives directly to Pacelli [Pope Pius XII].[167] Pacelli said that every one of his declarations should be seriously pondered and considered in the light of the interests of those persecuted, so that he would not make their circumstances even more difficult and unbearable. He wanted to say 'words of fire,' but the situation forced him into 'the silence of hope' to avoid reprisals."[168]

Invariably doubters who believe that the Roman Catholic Church was in league with the Nazis will also find that they have been ignoring totally the five million non-Jews who were victims of the Holocaust, over three million of whom were Polish Catholics.[169] There were numerous Catholic clergy from many conquered nations as well as German Jehovah's Witnesses and numerous other groups who were also victims of the Holocaust.

Alberto Rivera states then "a few years after he lost World War II, Pope Pius XII startled the world with his phoney [sic] dancing sun

---

[167] Pope Pius XII's name prior to being elected pope was Eugenio Pacelli. Spinosa refers to him by this name.
[168] "Historians Reveal Cornwell's Errors", Zenit News Agency, September 13, 1999
[169] Forgotten Holocaust: The Poles Under German Occupation 1939-1944, Richard C. Lukas, Hippocrene Books, 2001

vision to keep Fatima in the news." The most glaring falsehood here is that the Miracle of the Sun, the event that is referred to as the Pope's "phoney [sic] dancing sun vision" did not take place after the Second World War. It took place on October 13th, 1917, twenty-eight years before the end of the Second World War. Rivera then brashly says "not surprisingly, Pope Pius was the only one to see this vision." The plain truth is Pius XII was not even Pope at that time, only becoming pope on March 2nd, 1939, almost 22 years after the Miracle of the Sun had already taken place. And Pius was not even a witness to this event. But an estimated 70,000 Portuguese witnesses were reportedly present when this miracle took place.[170]

Whether one is ready to accept that this event was a miracle or whether it was something scientific or both, one cannot deny the testimonies of such a large number of witnesses who claimed to see this happening, including news reporters who were neutral observers and did not claim any religion.[171]

The Blue Army[172] of Our Lady of Fátima that Alberto Rivera mentions next is a Catholic lay society which was started in 1947 by Monsignor Harold V. Colgan and John M. Haffert. This group is focused on the spreading the message of Our Lady of Fátima in the United States and also worldwide as it was revealed in the visions of 1917. There is nothing paramilitary about this lay society. It simply

---

[170] The Sun's Miracle, or of Something Else?, Stanley L Jaki, Real View Books, 2000
[171] Fatima from the Beginning, John De Marchi, Ravengate Press, 1980
[172] Called "Blue Army of Our Lady of Fátima" or simply "Blue Army", deriving its name from Mary's liturgical color, blue.

encourages Eucharistic prayer and the rosary in "prayer cells", First Saturday devotions, family consecrations, and a Sacred Heart Home Enthronement Program. It is not an extremely missionary society, but more of an informative, encouragement society. The wording used in Rivera's testimony, "as a result, a group of followers has grown into the Blue Army world-wide [sic], totaling millions of faithful Roman Catholics ready to die for the blessed virgin", makes this group seem like a fanatical terrorist cell. As far as their being worldwide, the Blue Army operates a shrine in the New Jersey town of Washington, a town of nearly 7000 people, as well as a pilgrimage center in Fátima, Portugal.

Rivera continues on claiming that there were planned re-occurrences of Mary's appearance in Portugal in China, Russia as well as a "major appearance" in the United States. All of this is yet to be seen.

As well, the quotations attributed presumably to Archbishop Fulton J. Sheen have been neither cited by Jack Chick nor Alberto Rivera and have not been found by this author. But Archbishop Sheen did write something very similar in a 1952 book[173] about Mary in which he devoted a short chapter to converting Muslim's through the relationship between Mohammed's daughter Fatima and Mary choosing to reappear on earth in Portugal as Our Lady of Fátima. At the time Fulton was still a bishop and not yet elevated to archbishop.

---

[173] The World's First Love, Fulton J. Sheen, Garden City Books, 1952; and Ignatius Press, 1996. The text referred to is a chapter of the book called "Mary and the Moslems", later reprinted as a posthumous article: "The Power of Islam", Reverend Fulton J. Sheen, The Mindszenty Report, August, 1991.

Thus, *Bishop Sheen*, through his writing, seemed keen on the idea of using the Muslim reverence for both Fatima and Mary to bring them closer to Christianity.

This dream of Bishop Sheen's has not come to fruition. If it had come to fruition though, Alberto Rivera might just have found another conspiracy to sell...

The Religious Hoax of the Century?

By Leslie Price

Evangelicals Now, November 2000

The True Story of Alberto Rivera Uncovered

In a recent EN book review I expressed regret that the author had been taken in by the false claims of Alberto Rivera. An overseas reader asked for more details of what was perhaps the most successful religious literary hoax of the past century.

Alberto Rivera (1935-1997) was born and brought up in the Canary Islands where harassment of Protestants was much less than in mainland Spain.

His mother died when he was nine. As a teenager he left the Roman church and was baptised in the local evangelical church at 17. After working as a fare collector on the buses, in 1955 he independently obtained a place at a Protestant seminary in Costa Rica, but was expelled in 1957. For a time he worked for the Methodist Church in Costa Rica, and in 1964-5 for the Christian Re-formed Church in New Jersey, USA, who dismissed him.

Photographed as priest

In 1967 he returned to Spain where he was employed in a Christian school and again dismissed. He then secured work with children in a

Catholic parish. It was in this era that he had his photograph taken in priest's clothes on an identity card, and also obtained a certificate from the Archbishop of Madrid 'confirming' his status as a Catholic priest, which he was not.

In a brief visit to London in 1967, he encountered the Church of God in Prophecy and went to work with them in Tennessee, but was dismissed in 1968. He reappeared dressed as a priest in Puerto Rico in 1968, but returned to Florida in 1969 as a Protestant. In 1969 he functioned briefly as a priest in the Liberal Catholic Church, but left Florida suddenly and went to Seattle in Washington State. Eventually he ended up in California.

It was here that he established himself as an anti-Roman evangelist, and was also ordained as a Baptist minister. He claimed to have been a Jesuit agent, undermining Protestant churches, and to have knowledge of various atrocities, including murder, by Catholics. This message was carried around the world in millions of tracts.

Exposed as a fraud

Rivera was exposed a fraud in Christianity Today (March 13 1981) and in the Journal of Pastoral Practice the same year. He was exposed again in Forward (the magazine of the Christian Research Institute, USA) in 1983. Other exposures followed in Australia and South Africa - but some Canadian Protestants still believed in him. Roy Livesey, the British publisher of New Age Bulletin (to whom I am indebted for information) wrote a book, as yet unpublished, documenting the fraud.

In some ways Rivera was a typical confidence trickster. Accusations of theft, especially of money, constantly followed him, making a frequent change of address desirable. His employers (and, later, his employees), had cause to lament dearly the day he came to them. He usually had a hard luck story. He would tell the Protestants he had been persecuted by the Catholics or by a previous Protestant employer, and he told the Romans that he was a victim of the Protestants.

Evil faces

The Alberto tracts are notable examples of hate literature. The Roman Catholics in them have demonic faces, and apart from the absence of hooked noses could have stepped straight out of medieval anti-Jewish caricature, which eventually contributed to the Holocaust. There are stories of Catholics being converted by them, but for the more intelligent Catholic they simply show the malicious credulity of that church's critics.

The fraud is not a minor event. Even though Alberto never became well-known in the UK, the tracts have cascaded in millions among the barely literate of the Third World, poisoning the efforts of evangelical Christians to preach to Catholics. To support his stories, he also de-famed the evangelicals with whom while young he had been in fellowship, claiming to have subverted them. Those who exposed him, even members of his church, were accused of being Jesuit agents.

Still circulating

'The evil that men do lives after them', and the full extent of the damage may not be known for years. Alberto literature still circulates in the Protestant sub-culture, and widely in South America and the Third World where comic books are more appreciated.

Some of those who knew Alberto regard him as a paranoid schizophrenic. In the fantasies of those so afflicted, the Jesuits and the Roman Catholics often join the Masons, the Jews and intelligence agencies as favourite characters, along with exalted claims of being oneself an agent.

Looking back, those who had been deceived by Alberto sometimes paid tribute to his mesmerising plausibility. He took advantage both of the good will of Christians - their readiness to help those in need and also of Christian ill-will, the eagerness to credit evil to those who believed erroneously. Perhaps he was simply an evil person.

How the exposures were made

It is not easy to trace the movements of a man who lived in many countries. But in dealing with Alberto, Christians had two advantages.

First, Alberto was contemporary. It was possible, for example, to travel (as Roy Livesey did) to the Canary Islands and meet those who had known Alberto from his youth, to consult and copy photographs and other church records This left no doubt that he did not attend a Jesuit school. Spanish -speaking church members in Costa Rica and neighbouring countries could give personal testimony about the havoc he wrought. Which had nothing to do with his fantasy about being a Jesuit secret agent.

Secondly, Alberto's repeated changes of denomination left a paper trail across many church offices. Sometimes law enforcement agencies joined in, even the FBI, with vain attempts to get money back.

A typical document is a business card from 1973 issued by Alberto Magno R. Rivera (He had added the name Magno in later years.) He gives his degrees as D.T. D.D N.D. and DRH; by now he liked to be known as Dr Rivera. He also claimed at that time to be a Bishop in the Apostolic Catholic Church. The usual problems with unpaid bills soon brought this scam to an end.

And yet all the exposures in the world did not shut the Rivera fraud down. The tracts continue to be available, both to Christian bookstores, and now to anyone with a Web connection. At a time when the Church of Rome is very powerful, and Protestantism is in a parlous state here, some believers are still implicated in this wicked fraud. Where is the Christian discernment?

A typical story

'As I pulled the wood, the blanket unrolled, and I froze at what I saw. There were the bodies of seven little babies. Each had three crosses cut into their heads, a cross on each palm, and the bottoms of both feet, and on their chests were two large crosses. Their hearts were gone, the cross looked like this (diagram in original) which means the peace of Christ. I was so scared I couldn't speak.'

This is followed by another mutilation story involving a 13 year-old girl. The man who invented and spread these fantasies was clearly very disturbed. Christians would not usually allow them into their world, but here they have been smuggled in as anti-Catholic writings (from The Force).

Protestant dilemma

Typical of the problems caused by Rivera and others like him is a new booklet by Alan O'Reilly, Britain under Siege, published by Christian Concern, of Nuneaton.

This is an attack on the catastrophic decline of our nation as a Christian bulwark. Some of it comes from respected agencies like the Christian Institute or (on the secular side) The Social Affairs Unit.

But other material is derived from questionable sources, especially American writers who are grossly ignorant about the UK.

O'Reilly says of Rivera: 'The series encountered not only opposition from Rome but also from genuine but compromised Christian believers, trying to remain on friendly terms with the whore of Revelation.'

What do I do? I am very worried about the state of the nation. I take the Protestant faith to be based on Scripture, restated in the Reformation creeds, and in great peril today. I am not interested in being on friendly terms with the Church of Rome but I cannot go along with a malicious hoax.

This is not an isolated error. Having read the two-volume life of Bishop Westcott (in the Evangelical Library) I know also that statements made in the booklet about him are quite wrong. Because his biblical views are rejected, his life story is mangled.

All Protestant writers should avoid quoting American authors on British history unless they have checked the sources! In view of the immense numbers of heresies and cults which arise in the States, British writers should be especially on their guard against revelations from there.

From: "The Religious Hoax of the Century?" Leslie Price. Evangelicals Now, November 2000; Reprinted by permission. The text of the preceding article is copied directly from the original publication.

Alberto Rivera's False Anti-Catholic Story

(Plus "The Catholic Question," by the Cornerstone staff)

Is your name on a Vatican hit list?

Is the Catholic Church preparing a 20th-century Inquisition? Yes! Says Alberto Rivera, who claims to have been an espionage agent for the Catholic Church.

Alberto's testimony, entitled Alberto, is a "runaway best seller" published by Chick Publications, and is part of the "Crusader" comic book series. With the great success of Alberto, Jack Chick has now released a sequel entitled Double Cross.

Who Is Alberto Rivera and what is his message? Alberto tells us his story as follows: Spanish born, he was placed in a Jesuit seminary at the age of seven where he was trained for the priesthood. His Instructors taught him how to Infiltrate and destroy Protestant churches and aid the ecumenical movement. He claims he destroyed numerous Christian churches throughout the world. Then he was ordained a Jesuit priest and became a bishop. He says he worked with notable "Jesuit spies" such as Kathryn Kuhlman and Jim Jones. Because of his experience he was ordered to join the ecumenical forces under the Pope. There he says he learned that the Catholic Church had secretly joined forces with the Communists, the Masons, the Illuminati, and the charismatic movement. The hypocrisy of it all was too much for him. He began to expose what Rome was planning. For this he was committed to a sanitarium. There, on the verge of death, he was converted. Since he knew too much, the Catholic Church wanted him dead, but mysteriously he was released and helped out of Spain. He then rescued his sister, a nun, from death In a British convent. He now claims to be running for his life, hunted by Jesuit assassins.

The story has created tremendous controversy: the Christian Reformed Church, Zondervan Publishers, and the Southern Baptist Sunday School Board have banned it front their bookstores. As a result of the negative response to Alberto, Jack Chick has published a special, free promotional tract in its defense. In that tract, Jack Chick states that Christian bookstores are being infiltrated by undercover Catholic propaganda teams who pressure the owner until he "compromises with Rome and pulls Alberto out of the store." This is compared to "the few totally committed Gospel book stores" who carry his books "because they see it is the only effective soul winning book to win Catholics that's published today."

In support of the book's truthfulness, on January 30, 1980, Alberto Rivera issued a sworn statement defending his allegations. Rivera declared, in part, " 'Alberto' is a true and actual account, and I will face a court ot [sic) law to prove the events actually took place. I hereby challenge anyone who would refute or try to prove the facts and information in this book are untrue." Recently, the Catholic League for Religious and Civil Rights has asked the California

Attorney General's office to investigate Jack T. Chick and Alberto Rivera for "false advertising and consumer fraud."

Is Alberto's story true? No! Our intensive investigation reveals his police record, his investment schemes, his bad check☐writing, his contradictory testimony, his fabricated educational record, and his reported family abuse.

Alberto Rivera, also known as Alberto Romero, has a history of legal entanglements. He is currently involved in a court action In Southern California, accused of fraud. According to Cesar Ramirez, he gave Alberto over $2,000 to Invest In some property in Huntington Park, California. The property was never purchased. When Mr. Ramirez asked for his money back, Alberto gave him a donation slip for $2,000 Ramirez has now sued him to recover his money.

In 1965, a warrant for his arrest was issued in Hoboken, New Jersey, for writing bad checks. He also left debts in excess of $3,000.

In October, 1967, Alberto went to work at the Church of God of Prophecy headquarters In Tennessee. Alberto began collecting funds for a college in Tarrassa, Spain. When the Church of God of Prophecy wrote the college to see if he was authorized to collect funds on their behalf, the church received the following reply: the college had given him a letter to collect funds, but only for the month of July. The school later discovered that while he "claimed to be a Catholic priest ... he had never been one." They reported he left debts which he had drawn in the name of the parish of San Lorenzo, and that the Spanish police were seeking him for "authentic swindles and cheats." Finally, they said no funds he raised had ever reached the college.

In a letter to the Department of Justice, Rev. Charles Hawkins of the Church of God of Prophecy stated Alberto's bank had contacted them because he had written a check to Delta Air Lines on a closed account. In 1969 two warrants were issued against him in DeLand and Ormond Beach, Florida. The first was for the theft of a Bank□Americard. The criminal Investigation division of the Bank of America reports he charged over $2,000 on the credit card. The second warrant was for the 'unauthorized use of an automobile." Alberto abandoned the vehicle in Seattle, Washington. From there he moved to Southern California.

Alberto's account of his conversion is contradictory. In 1964 while working for the Christian Reformed Church, he said he was converted from Catholicism in July of 1952. Now he maintains it was in 1967. While speaking at the Faith Baptist Church in Canoga Park, California, Alberto pinpointed his conversion at 3:00 in the morning on March 20, 1967. He says he immediately defected from the Catholic Church. However, five months later, in August of 1967, he was still promoting Catholicism and the ecumenical movement in a newspaper interview in his hometown of Las Palmas in the Canary Islands. Another discrepancy involves his three month stay in a sanitarium. In Alberto, he says he was placed in a sanitarium in 1965 for exposing the Catholic Church. This would put his "conversion" and release from the sanitarium no later than April, 1966. The book Alberto lists his release as September, 1967. Alberto doesn't reveal what happened during those one and a half years. However, in the newspaper interview in Las Palmas (August 1967), he said he had been doing ecumenical work in Tarrassa, Spain, during the previous 6 months (Feb.□Aug. 1967). This is the time he was supposed to be in a sanitarium for exposing Rome's ecumenical plot!

PRIESTHOOD

Alberto's claim to have been a Jesuit priest and bishop are denied by the Catholic Church. They state that the document he exhibits as proof of his priesthood is little more than a form letter giving permission to travel abroad. The document was fraudulently obtained. Alberto's accounts of his ordination are contradictory. In 1967 when Alberto was visiting his family in Las Palmas, he said he had been ordained a priest in Costa Rica; in 1978, while at the Faith Baptist Church in Canoga Park, California, he said he was ordained In Las Palmas.

Alberto now claims that he was once a Jesuit bishop. None of his format associates remember this being part of his testimony until the early 19703. Former associate Rev. Wishart (once a pastor of the First Baptist Church of San Fernando), who questioned Alberto about this, reported that Alberto admitted that he had never been ordained a bishop, but used the title for prestige. He continues to call himself the bishop of his own church, the Hispanic Baptist Church (Oxnard, CA).

After Alberto allegedly escaped the Catholics in Madrid, DoubleCross devotes nine pages to the rescue and conversion of his sister "Maria," a nun, from a convent in London. Alberto was in London during the time mentioned in the comic (Sept. 1967), but was staying at a Catholic monastery rather than the YMCA described in Double☐Cross. Rev. Delmar Spurling (Church of God of Prophecy) picked him up at the monastery, and attests that Alberto had only one sister in London: her name wasn't Maria, she wasn't a nun, and didn't live in a convent, but in a private London home as a maid. Alberto stayed with Church of God of Prophecy members for approximately a month until his return to the U.S.

DIPLOMA MILL DEGREES

Alberto commands great respect from many with his alleged numerous degrees including an N.D., a D.D., a Th.D., a Ph.D., and a master's in psychology. However, he is ambiguous when asked where he received these degrees. Alberto attended a seminary in Costa Rica (the Seminario Biblio Latinamericano) with a friend from Las Palmas, but he did not graduate. That friend, Rev. Plutarco Bonilla (a respected Christian leader in Central America), said that Alberto never finished high school in Las Palmas and that he was in the seminary's program for non☐high school graduates. The school in a letter said they were forced to expel Alberto for his "continual lying and defiance of seminary authority," The known chronology of his life does not allow time for him to have achieved the academic status he claims. When Rev. Wishart pressed Alberto concerning his degrees, Alberto admitted receiving them from a diploma mill in Colorado. This ended their relationship. Pastor Rassmussen (Faith Baptist Church in Canoga Park, California) also asked Alberto to substantiate some of his claims by submitting to a lie detector test. Alberto said he would: three limes appointments were made for him; three times he failed to appear.

Alberto's past family relationships have been described negatively by those who knew them. He met his first "wife" in Costa Rica while working with the Methodist church. Rev. Bonilla says that Alberto was living there with a woman in the late 1950s but they weren't legally married: Alberto said God ordained their marriage. Alberto later claimed in an employment form that he and Carmen Lydia Torres were married on November 25, 1963. Their son Juan was born in Hoboken, New Jersey, in September, 1964, where Alberto was working with the Christian Reformed Church. A supervisor at the time, Rev. Edson Lewis, said that Alberto physically abused both Carmen Lydia and Juan. Less than a year after his birth, in July, 1965, Juan died in El Paso, Texas, where his parents had fled, after they wrote bad checks in New Jersey.

His marriage relationship to Carmen Lydia was further complicated as described in the letter by Rev. Charles Hawkins (Church of God of Prophecy In Tennessee) to the U.S. Department of Justice. The letter stated that Alberto and Carmen Lydia's wedding was scheduled in

Tennessee in 1968, but that Carmen Lydia missed the wedding, staying in Puerto Rico instead.

Alberto then went to Puerto Rico and returned to the States with a new son, Alberto. Carmen Lydia followed them a few months later. This is according to former associate and roommate Rev. Daniel Abrego, who added that Alberto had left Carmen Lydia in Mexico when he returned to Spain in 1966. It is difficult to determine the whereabouts of the child Alberto today, but Rev. Abrego claims he was placed in a welfare home in Tennessee. They didn't have a child with them when they went to Florida in 1969.

Alberto and Carmen Lydia had still another son, Luis Marx, early in 1969. While they were in Florida, their hosts said Luis Marx was mistreated. What happened to Luis Marx is unknown, but when Alberto left Florida for Seattle with the car and credit card they no longer had the child with them. What happened to Carmen Lydia after Seattle is also unknown, but Alberto remarried in 1977 to Nury Frias, a woman, from the Dominican Republic. Whether he was ever legally married to and/or divorced from the other woman is unknown. At any rate, it is extremely damaging to Rivera's credibility to discover that he had two children (Juan and Alberto) in America during the time he was supposed to be a celibate priest in Europe!

PAST AND PRESENT

Alberto Is known to have been affiliated with: the Methodist church, the Church of Christ, the Christian Reformed Church, the Church of God of Prophecy, and various Pentecostal and Baptist churches, as well as the controversial Universal Life Church. He has formed a number of organizations: Agapesofia Oikoumene, the Catholic Apostolic Church, the Hispanic Baptist Church (of Oxnard), and most recently the Antichrist Information Center. While Alberto claims the Antichrist Information Center is a tax☐exempt, non☐profit organization, the IRS denies it. He has also requested in his newsletter that donors not send cash because the Knights of Columbus postal employees are opening his mail.

He now lives in Ontario, California; he owns a church in Oxnard, and a service station☐grocery store in Northern California, as well as some undeveloped properties. He is gathering funds for an alleged hide☐away retreat for ex-priests and nuns and is asking for $110,000 more to complete this project.

What does Jack Chick think about this? It's hard to find out, because he has made it a policy not to speak with reporters. But when he was finally reached by phone at his home, he said that he had never met a more godly man than Alberto, and that he knows Alberto's story is true because he ,.prayed about it." Jack says he expects his own life to be taken by Jesuit assassins.

When we reached Alberto by phone, he also refused to meet with us. (Alberto has an office in the Chick Publications headquarters.) He claims that any wrongdoings prior to his conversion in 1967 were done under the orders of the Catholic Church, and any wrongdoings since his conversion are fabrications by the conspirators.

As we have seen, Alberto's story is fraudulent, as was the story of John Todd, another Jack Chick protégé, who said the witches are taking over the world (see Issue 148 of Cornerstone). Alberto has skillfully created a closed, paranoid defense system which makes it difficult to corner him on specific issues. He can always dismiss any accusation as part of the Jesuit plot.

Is Jack naive or is he publishing these stories because they are big sellers? It's impossible to know what his motives are, but after the John Todd fiasco, he should have withdrawn those publications and should have been much more careful before publishing another sensationalistic testimony.

How should we respond? First, we need to be more discerning about what we read and what stories we promote. We should not succumb to "last days paranoia." God has promised to bring us through every situation. Last, we need to pray: for Christians who have accepted his story and are now suspicious of other Christians, for Jack Chick that he will be more responsible with his publications, and for Alberto that he will truly repent and follow Christ. *

Gary Metz has written several articles for Cornerstone □ "Conspiracy or Conspirator?: The John Todd Story" in Issue 48; "Angels on

Assignment: Fact or Fiction?" in Issue 50; and "is Christianity a Cult?" and "Jimmy Swaggart" (regarding contemporary Christian music) in Issue 51. In addition to this article, which was funded by and researched initially for Cornerstone, the information in "The Alberto story" will be found in an upcoming issue of Christianity Today, Gary is currently working with a research organization in California.

If you have any further information about Alberto Rivera, or it you desire additional clarification regarding his story, please write to: Gary Metz c/o C.A.R.I.S. P.O. Box 1783 Santa Ana, CA 92702

The Catholic Question

Alberto Rivera's fraudulent claims underscore a sad fact: many Protestants have as distorted a view of Catholics as whites earlier in the century had of blacks. The black man was caricatured as having "lotsa rhythm and little□a brains," while the Catholic is portrayed as an automaton who is in unquestioning bondage to church authorities.

In understanding Catholics, we must dispense with the picture of a pre□Reformation "Mother Church." The Catholic Church today is an amalgamation of 'traditional, liberal, and evangelical theology.

Vatican 1/ (1962□1965) had much to do with this. No longer were Protestants "accursed"; we became "separated brethren." Some priests openly denied papal infallibility (an official church doctrine) but were barely even chastised for it. Liberal theologians made an impact, though there were limits to Catholic elasticity. (Theologian Hans Kung, after echoing the teachings of Karl Barth's neo☐orthodox theology, recently was forbidden to teach.)

As the decade of the sixties progressed, and mainline Protestant churches were brought to new life by a latter☐day Pentecost, a parallel movement occurred within Catholic circles. Called "the charismatic movement," Its effect became so strong that Cardinal Joseph Suenens was chosen by Pope Paul VI as a sympathetic overseer.

For a time, the names "Catholic" and "Protestant" became secondary to the fervent mutual experience of God's grace. It was common to see Protestant/Catholic prayer groups and Bible studies spring up over night. Evangelicals' eyes widened at the sight of Catholics toting a large study Bible wherever they went, a Bible as well marked as their own.

Our relationship towards Catholicism should not echo the left and right, to and fro, veering of society's opinion. The conservative swing of our country, as positive as it is, in many respects comes with the potential for a reactionary pride totally absent from Scripture. It is this pride, the naive arrogance of "being right," that would erect walls between us and our Catholic brothers and sisters. This "spirit of the age" is one which discourages innovation and reaching out, encouraging retreat and fortification.

153

We needn't accept Catholic doctrine to embrace Catholic Christians. Let us be informed concerning our doctrinal differences and use that intelligence in a good way. A spiritually aware Catholic will be as honest as any one of us and won't brush doctrine aside.

As one Catholic priest, Father Kenneth Ryan, writes: "There can be no true and complete unity in Christ until we know Christ as he really is ... Doctrine is important because it is truth, and love which is not based on truth will hardly endure."

Protestants should understand the Reformational truths of the primacy of Scripture, justification by faith, and the priesthood of the believer. Catholic doctrines such as transubstantiation (the idea that in communion, the bread and wine in actuality become the blood and body of Christ), the sacrificial nature of the Mass (Christ, in one sense, again is sacrificed for our sins), the exalted role of Mary, and the intercessory role of the Saints all must be subjected to Scriptural scrutiny by the Protestant believer.

To deliberate concerning our faith is not a denial of truth; it is an affirmation of it. In short, we must agree with evangelical author John Stott, who says, "I find myself hoping and praying that evangelicals worldwide will take more initiatives to develop friendly conversations with Roman Catholics based on common Bible study. It would be tragic indeed if God's purpose of reformation were frustrated by our evangelical stand offishness."

In conclusion, we cannot be the judge of our brother's motives for staying in, or coming out, of the Catholic Church. All Catholics are not born□again Christians, and the large majority of charismatic and evangelical Catholics have elected to remain within their church as a seed of hope, much like those evangelicals who are attempting to renew the mainline Protestant denominations. God requires nothing more or less of us for them than our support, our friendship, and our prayers.

From: "The Alberto Story," Gary Metz. Cornerstone Magazine, vol. 9, no. 53, 1981, pp. 29-31; Reprinted by permission. The text of the preceding article is copied directly from the original publication.

ALBERTO RIVERA, REVEALOR OF SECRETS

OR

SPANISH SVENGALI, TELLER OF TALES?

And I looked, and, lo, a Lamb stood on the mount Sion, and with him an hundred forty and four thousand, having his Father's name written in their foreheads......and in their mouth was found no guile: for they are without fault before the throne of God."

March 1, 2003

Dear Jack Chick:

It has been years since I reviewed my Alberto comics, Parts 1-5, all of which include his testimony as an ex-Jesuit Priest under the Extreme Oath. I was compelled to do so recently because there are several Christians who testify that Mr. Rivera's personal history is fiction. One gentleman has even written an unauthorized biography of Rivera, at his own expense, as yet unpublished, though he sent the manuscript to you. The author declares Alberto's claims do not coincide with reality.

As part of my recent research I listened to two audio tapes. The first was produced by Rivera himself, upon Walter Martin's visit accompanied by his assistant, Brian Onken, taking place in the early 80's, I believe. The second was taped off the air on May 30, 1990, when Alberto was interviewed on KRBT radio, Los Angeles.

But I say unto you that every idle word that men shall speak, they shall give account thereof in the Day of Judgment. For by thy words thou shalt be justified, and by thy words thou shalt be condemned. (Matt. 12:36-37)

In the radio interview, Alberto was asked a straight-forward question regarding his many alleged credentials. He claimed seven degrees, which is why he calls himself, 'Dr.' Rivera. Yet, on air, before thousands of listeners, he could list only six:

Doctor of Philosophy
Doctor of Theology
Doctor of Sociology
Doctor of History
Doctor of Bible
Master of Psychology

Furthermore, he adamantly stated, several times, that he received his first doctorate in 1947. The rest, he claimed, he received over the next 9 years or so. Unfortunately, he admitted, he had no way of proving that fact, which he attempted to explain by way of a kind of thick, garbled, Spanish-Anglo doubletalk. Quite frankly, his English was so poor it was difficult for me to believe he had even attained a high school diploma, let alone six or seven doctorates. Later in the same program, a caller, using elementary mathematics, computed Rivera to be 12 years old when he received his Ph.D.! Alas, Rivera was again forced to manifest his uncanny natural ability of double-talking his way out of an extremely uncomfortable situation. Curiously, though he began the radio interview by stating he had no tangible proof of his many earned degrees, yet by the end of the program he confessed to having 190 documents which 'prove' who he is.

If that is true, Mr. Chick, why have you not published them?

My conclusion, after listening to the two audio tapes which attempted to delve into Rivera's personal history - the interviewers using Rivera himself as their primary source - is that he is a master manipulator, ever changing the subjects at hand by whispering in hushed, urgent, thick, garbled Spanish-Anglo tones, "Now I want you listen very carefully what I going to say......".

Nowhere in the Alberto comics do I find reference to the years of study Alberto must have undergone to attain such highly regarded credentials. According to the Jesuits themselves:

Commonly Asked Questions

Q: How long does it take to become a Jesuit?

A: Once a man finishes the two-year novitiate, he takes vows of poverty, chastity and obedience either as a Jesuit brother or as a scholastic who will prepare for ordination. At this time, the man is

considered a Jesuit. On the average, it takes about nine more years of study and work before scholastics are ordained priests and brothers complete their formation.
http://www.jesuit.org/sections/sub.asp?SECTION_ID=189&SUBSECTION_ID=431&PARENT_ID=234

Where are those 9 years of blood, sweat and tears, in which he is heavily preoccupied in Jesuitical studies in order to receive minimal scholastic standing in the Order? Did they begin at age 16 when he was apparently first informed that Peter, not Christ, was the Rock upon whom the Church is built? But was not Alberto too busy infiltrating and destroying hundreds of Protestant churches and organizations to complete the heavy scholastic workload necessary for ordination? Let's face it, if, in fact, Alberto were to gain the feigned trust of others, does that not take quite some time and effort? To infiltrate and destroy ONE church would be a major undertaking.....but HUNDREDS, all the while studying for SEVEN graduate degrees?! Mr. Chick, how long did it take before an employee of yours attained 'trustworthy status' to where he gained your confidence, having access to your ear? A week, a month, a year, or more? Now multiply that by 'hundreds.' Do you not see the improbability of such an absurd claim? And have you ever pursued graduate studies? Do you think the average graduate student has time for many outside activities, let alone ESPIONAGE ASSIGNMENTS taking him around the world? Do you not see the improbability of such an absurd claim?

When this present writer became a Christian in January, 1989, by the sovereign grace of God, I spent nine years, FULL-TIME, in preparation for this ministry. I ate, drank and slept the Word of God the entire time, and I have witnesses to prove it. And even today my studies still continue (and will continue until my last breath). In other words, it is no easy task to be knowledgeable in biblical subjects to the point of being ready to teach others. But to claim SEVEN graduate degrees PLUS hundreds of espionage assignments, worldwide, in as short a time span claimed by Rivera is so far-fetched as to indicate an innate pathological disorder.

My question to you, Mr. Chick: Why on earth did you turn off your critical thinking, your ability to discern truth from lies, facts from fiction? In other words, where was your common sense, man?

Let me cite you a few more examples in Alberto's testimony which cried out, WARNING, WARNING!!, if only you had ears to hear.

In the mouth of two or three witnesses every word may be established. (Matt. 18:16)

Surely, Mr. Rivera had known this simple Bible principle BEFORE allegedly leaving the Jesuit Order. The more fantastic the claims of the witness, the greater the quality and quantity of proof necessary to substantiate the claims. Christ's claims were extraordinary, but His proofs were equally extraordinary, in both substance and number. In like manner, Rivera, a man with seven graduate degrees could not be

160

ignorant that he needed substantial proofs regarding his history with the Jesuits, as well as his testimony as to the TRUE, BUT SECRET HISTORY OF THE WORLD.

But alas, we have no corroborating evidence of his membership in the Society of Jesus. As a man who came from a Spanish Roman Catholic family, he must have had numerous brothers, sisters, cousins, aunts and uncles. Surely, one could have come forward to testify on his behalf. But none have come forward. Why not? Were they all afraid of reprisals by the Jesuits? Or did they prefer to distance themselves from their relative's embarrassingly tall tales? Even his sister, Maria, whom he allegedly rescued from an evil convent, did not do Alberto the courtesy of publicly confirming his story. Instead, she marries a traitor and disappears! How tragic, but at the same time, how convenient.

Furthermore, was the Lord ignorant of the necessity to back up Alberto's fantastic claims with other reputable witnesses? Of course not. Then, why, pray tell, did He not bring another Jesuit out of the Society, by the same omnipotent power He used to bring Alberto out? Was His power exhausted? Or perhaps He miscalculated the controversy over Alberto's lack of credentials and his innumerable, unsubstantiated claims, the Lord somehow neglecting to provide those essential two or three corroborating witnesses? Like his sister, Maria, ALL other ex-Jesuits, Alberto tells us, "are either in hiding, disappeared or dead." Thus, the lack of one corroborating witness. Again, how convenient.

At the last came two false witnesses. (Matt. 26:60) Moreover, in The Godfathers, Alberto, Part Three, and other Alberto editions, he declares secret knowledge of world history as taught to him and his Jesuit compatriots in special Vatican 'briefings' under the tutelage of Augustin Cardinal Bea. Incredibly, though Rivera paints, in every color imaginable, the Jesuits as dissemblers of the highest order, never to be trusted, men would murder at the slightest provocation, his ONLY SOURCE for this incredulous re-telling of world history is the German Jesuit, Cardinal Bea! Not even Edmund Paris nor the revered Reverend Alexander Hislop were privy to the amazing behind-the-scene truths of history which Alberto had been so privileged to reveal to the ignorant Christians, scholars and historians of our Age!

Certainly, revelations of this magnitude should require an Angel of the Lord on special assignment from God Almighty. Even Joseph Smith was wise enough to include visits from the Angel Moroni, as well as manifestations of God the Father and Son to him personally before he began to claim divine prophet status. But alas, all we have from Alberto is his unsubstantiated say-so that Cardinal Bea allegedly said so, and what this arch enemy of the saints said so is God's truth. Rivera uses a Jesuit master of deceit as his reliable and trustworthy source. Incredible. "I read it in the archives in the Vatican." Alberto asserts access to 'secret files' in the Vatican archives. Any person with a minimal knowledge of the Middle Ages and earlier Church history is cognizant that the vast majority of Church documents were written in Latin, the official language of the Roman Catholic Church. Thus, we have another problem. Rivera knew no Latin, with the exception of a few stock phrases. Donald Blanton, Rivera's close associate at AIC for a number of years, testifies to contacting ex-priest, Robert Champagne, for his assistance in translating Latin documents, due to the fact of Rivera's woeful deficiency in that area. There was even talk of Mr. Champagne's joining the AIC ministry, though it was not to be. Mr. Chick, I speak from personal experience in Latin translations. Our ministry uses the gracious services of an ex-priest who teaches college level Latin courses. He has been doing this for years and, though quite gifted, even HE has difficulty in translating Latin Church documents from the Middle Ages for use by our ministry

By the way, Rivera's re-telling of the riveting, true story of Donna Maria de Bohorques, came by way of reading Juan Antonio Llorente's classic, A Critical History of the Inquisition of Spain, pp. 216-218, not from reading the mile-long, secret, underground Latin files on the Dominicans.

ALBERTO'S ESCHATOLOGY

And lastly, although Alberto proudly boasts of intimate 'insider' knowledge of all the inner workings and covert schemes of the Vatican and Jesuit Order, knowledge which NONE of his heroes, the Protestant Reformers, claimed to have, he makes the unforgivable omission of informing Christians regarding paramount knowledge the

Reformers DID have. I speak of the well-documented fact that it was the Jesuits Bellarmine and Ribera who propagated Futurism, and the Jesuits Alcazar and Bossuet who propagated Preterism, the two false schools of prophetic teaching whose purpose was to destroy the biblical Protestant teaching that it is the current Pope of Rome who is the great Antichrist, and we are to look for no other.....not even at the end of the world. In this the Jesuits were highly successful, which can be proved by a cursory examination of Evangelical prophetic websites on the WWW.

There can only be two reasons Rivera neglected this most important historical fact. (1) The Holy Spirit is not his Teacher; and (2) His eschatology leans toward Jesuit Futurism. Rivera mixes Jesuit Futurism into his eschatology by prophesying a future Holocaust of Christians, a future Great Tribulation, a future One World Church, a future One World Government, led by a future Pope at the end of the world whom Satan will indwell, making him the Man of Sin, the Antichrist.

Never mind the errors of known, factual history contained in the comic books which can be refuted by several unbiased sources. Nor do we need examine the testimony of those who knew him, who worked closely with him, testimony damning to his Christian character and ethic. No, we needn't look that far to determine the credibility of this 'Christian' teacher. They are all liars anyway, according to Alberto, traitors to the cause, Jesuit infiltrators sent by the enemy.

Mr. Chick, the saga of Alberto......the man who witnessed a fellow priest sliced into pieces by demons while Catholics hovered in the air; .....the man who experienced the tortures of a padded cell in an insane asylum especially designed for obstinate priests, unable to sleep because of incessant propaganda piped in through a wall speaker; ......the man who was heavily drugged, having been given numerous shock treatments, only to find himself ensconced in an iron lung, from which he miraculously escapes, healed by the power of God; ......the man who is then inexplicably given permission to leave the country to find freedom, but who then risks his life in saving his precious sister from imprisonment under the rule of a coven of wicked nuns; ....the man whom the Vatican placed on their Death Wish List; .....the man whom the Jesuits failed to kill, though they threw him in front of a London subway, though the IRA blew up his residence in Ireland, though they managed to place ground glass in his food while attending a prayer meeting, though they shot at him at least 5 times, and though his dentist, a Jesuit agent, sprayed him with nerve gas, leaving an instrument inside his tooth with the hopes of an infection reaching his brain, thereby causing death; .....The man who was finally laid to rest six years ago when Jesuit agents successfully introduced a slow-working poison ......this man and the story of his life will remain one of the more memorable examples of the STRONG DELUSION sent by the Lord upon the lovers of lies.

Mr. Chick, as a Christian answerable to the Church and her Head, the Lord Jesus Christ, I beseech you to cease printing and distributing these God-dishonoring fables. Those true saints and martyrs who are honored for their courageous stand against the papal Antichrist have NO GUILE found in their mouths, unlike Mr. Rivera. I also request that you publicly repent, asking forgiveness for your having come under the spell of a Spanish Svengali, and false prophet.

Rand Winburn
Director
Protestant Reformation Publications
http://www.iconbusters.com

Reprinted by permission. The text of the preceding article is copied directly from the original publication.

Interview with Dr. Walid Mustafa

On the 23rd or June, 2006, I had the privilege of interviewing Dr. Walid Mustafa, Associate Professor in the Department of Humanities at the La Sallian school Bethlehem University of the Holy Land. Since 2004 Dr. Mustafa has been Dean of Faculty of the Arts. Previously he was Dean of Students at the same university. Dr. Mustafa received his Ph.D. from Kiev State University in the Ukraine. He has authored or co-authored several books and numerous articles about various aspects of geography, history, society and politics in the region. Bethlehem University of the Holy Land, or simply Bethlehem University, is located in the town of Bethlehem in the West Bank region of the Palestinian state.

Gary Dale: *Dr. Mustafa, I appreciate the opportunity to interview you and I am very happy to have the chance to gain more background about some of the incredible claims in Alberto Rivera's account of how the Roman Catholic Church allegedly helped to "create" Islam. Can you begin by telling me a little bit about the Jews of the Arabian Peninsula who were contemporaries of the prophet Mohammed?*

Dr. Mustafa: The Jews who lived in this land were of Arab origin. They spoke Arabic and they had Arab names. Their traditions were those of the Arabian Peninsula. Judaism, like Islam and Christianity, is not a nationality. Nor does it mark tribal or national affiliation as is known. A man may be Buddhist and still belong to his homeland India, Thailand, or China. Similarly, a man may belong to Judaism and have an Arab, Russian or French nationality.

<u>Gary Dale</u>: *Can you provide a little background on where these Jews came from? What was their history?*

<u>Dr. Mustafa</u>: When Moses and his followers in Judaism emigrated from Egypt to the land of the Canaanites, the present holy land, archeological studies, including the Israeli's, that is critical of the Torah-historical school, proved that the number of those who emigrated from Egypt was limited and that that emigration did not take place in thousands. Therefore, Judaism gradually spread to a part of the Canaanite tribes living in those lands. The proof for this is that the state established by Saul, David and Solomon did not come into being at once but after about three centuries after the emigration of the followers of Moses to the holy land. Had the emigration been in thousands, when population of the holy land ranged between 50 and 100 thousand, the Jewish state would not have taken that long to be established.

The facts of archeological studies show that this Jewish state was a part of small political entities, known as city states or tribal cities that were established in the Canaanite land in the 11th century BC. These small states came into being simultaneously in the Canaanite land, namely Philistia, Phoenicia, Aram, Amon, Adom, and the kingdom of Judea, which soon was divided during the reign of Rahba'am (Solomon's son) into the kingdoms of Judea and Israel. Those six "states" shared their origins, dialects (Semitic languages) and cultural standard. It is difficult to distinguish between the archeological and cultural remains of those states. In other words, the Jewish kingdom was not an alien body, established by aliens in the land but it was established by a group who lived in this region and constituted a part of its history. Consequently, there exists no nationalist ties between the Jews of the world and the kingdom that was established in the 11th century. In fact, the ties between them are spiritual, similar to those that link the Christians with Bethlehem, Jerusalem and Nazareth in the holy land and the Muslim with Mecca, Medina and Jerusalem. No Christian or Muslim in the world can claim that he has nationalist ties with Saudi Arabia or Palestine, which give him the right to citizenship, dominion or sovereignty. This land has its nationals that are attached to it historically and nationally.

Gary Dale: *You just mentioned that the Jews were emigrating back from Egypt over a long period of time and gradually built up their state. How then did they get so spread out throughout the Holy Land as well as outside of the region after that?*

Dr. Mustafa: Some citizens in this state, as was the case in other kingdoms, spread in the adjacent regions through what was known in that era, the ten centuries before Christ, as captivity. The victorious or conquerors from Mesopotamia or the Nile used to capture the most beautiful, skilled strongest among the defeated nation and take them to Babel and other capitals of the conquering nations, in order to participate in rebuilding, developing and serving those capitals. Some of those used to return home later on or remain in the new country. This happened with the Jews, who were taken into captivity by Nebuchadnezzar in the 6th century before Christ.

<u>Gary Dale</u>: *This is how Jews got to Mesopotamia. Alberto Rivera speaks specifically of Jews in Arabia. Could you elaborate a little about how the Jews got to Arabia?*

<u>Dr. Mustafa</u>: A part of the followers of Judaism who lived in the Holy Land during the Greek and Roman reigns moved to the adjacent regions in the Northern Arabian Peninsula (the city of Yathrib, including the Khaibar village) and to the Southern Peninsula (Yemen), due to the tyranny of the new regimes that did not accept Judaism as a competitor to the official religion of the ruling government. Some of them my have moved of their own will in search for new more favorable means of living in an area other than the homeland, as was the case of the nations of that epoch. This helped in the spread of Judaism in one way or another among the nations of the new regions, which were of Arab origins, to which the Jews emigrated.

<u>Gary Dale</u>: *How about Mohammed's relations with the Jews? Was he known to have contact with Jews in the Arabian Peninsula?*

<u>Dr. Mustafa</u>: After the severe ordeal experienced by Prophet Mohammad and his followers at the hands of the leaders of Mecca, he accepted the invitation extended to him and his followers to emigrate to the city of Yathrib,[174] which lies to the south of Mecca and which

---

[174] Yathrib today is known in Arabic as "Madinat Al-Nabi" (City of the Prophet). In English the city is commonly called "Medina".

was considered the second city in importance in the Peninsula at that time. The Jews of Yathrib and Khaibar participated in welcoming Mohammad and his compatriots. However, the establishment of the Islamic state in Yathrib later on and its growing stronger in power led to conflict with the commercial and social interests of the Arab Jewish leaders in Yathrib, which led to eruption of armed struggle with the two parties and the defeat of the Jews. This forced a number of them to leave the North of the Arabian Peninsula, heading to the Holy Land, Iraq, Yemen and Egypt, either by force or willingly. After the completion of the victory of the Islamic state in the Arabian Peninsula, a law was issued, which forbade followers of other religions to live in the cities of Mecca and Yathrib. They could reside in the other cities and regions of the Peninsula.

Gary Dale: *The assertion by Alberto Rivera through Jack Chick's tract comic The Prophet claims that the Vatican used Islam to extinguish Jews and rival Christian, non-Catholic denominations. Can you give us some background as to how the Christians, and Jews, were treated in the area as Islam became the dominant religion of the area?*

Dr. Mustafa: When Islam spread in what is called the Middle East at the beginning of the 7th century, the followers of Judaism and Christianity living in that region were clearly protected. Their religious places and properties were also protected. Use was made of their experiences in administrative matters, the sciences, translation and literature. Followers of Judaism and Christianity lived in peace

171

and cooperation with the new Islamic state and many of them were distinguished as men of politics, science, literature and art.

Gary Dale: *And how about North Africa and the Iberian Peninsula?*

Dr. Mustafa: When the Muslim Arabs conquered northern Africa and the Iberian Peninsula (Andalusia), the Jewish Arabs moved with them and emerged as a part of the political entities that were established in that land. When the Arab Muslims were defeated in Andalusia at the end of the 15th century AD, the Muslim, Jewish and Christian Arabs moved to the northern part of Africa and other regions of the Ottoman state. Some Jews lived in the northern part of Africa (Morocco, Algeria, Tunisia and Libya), forming a large Arab Jewish community there. Some others moved to Egypt, Turkey, Greater Syria and Iraq, joining the Jews who were originally living there.

Gary Dale: *And although the Jews have been spinning out of the Holy Land for centuries before, it is still safe to say that an important part of the Jewish Diaspora started and was closely tied in with the spread of Islam, rather than the claims that Jews and Christians were "put under the sword", so to speak. In the Rivera story this doesn't fit because Alberto Rivera claims that there has been animosity stirred between the Jews and the Arabs by the Vatican since basically the birth of Islam. Can you elaborate on when and where you believe the animosity arose?*

<u>Dr. Mustafa</u>: It should be noted that throughout history, Jewish communities moved to Europe via the Persian and Caucasian lands and that community contributed to the spread of Judaism among the different European nations. Arab Jews enjoyed continued living in peace and cooperation with their fellow Christian and Muslim Arabs in most of the Arab countries until the establishment of the state of Israel in 1948, when the tragic events that befell the Palestinian people, who paid a heavy price that led to the emigration and evacuation of more than 750,000 Palestinians out of their villages and cities on which Israel was established. That led to spread of an atmosphere of suspicion and hatred, which were used by the Zionist movement, which conducted a wide propaganda campaign that led to the emigration of the vast majority of the Arab Jews from Morocco, Algeria, Tunisia, Libya, Egypt, Iraq, Syria, Lebanon and Yemen. The number of Jews of Arab origin is estimated to be between 30 and 35% of the population of Israel at present. A visitor to Israel can notice the clinging of those Arab Jews to the customs, traditions and culture that they carried with them from the Arab countries out of which they emigrated. Those residents may serve as a bridge that leads to the achievement of a just and comprehensive peace between Arabs and Jews.

<u>Gary Dale</u>: *If you don't mind, I would like to turn our attention now to Waraqah, who is sort of portrayed as an agent of the Roman Catholic Church in Alberto Rivera's testimony. Can you give me some background on him?*

Dr. Mustafa: Waraqah was the uncle or cousin of Khadijah bint Khuwaylid, the first wife of the Prophet. Waraqah witnessed their wedding.

Gary Dale: *Can you give me an idea of Waraqah's religious background?*

Dr. Mustafa: Waraqah ibn Nawfal was a Christian. He didn't inherit this from his parents but reached this out of personal conviction. He traveled to Damascus, met there a number of Christians and then followed this religion. Before Islam, Waraqah was known by the Arabs as a member of a group named "Hanafiyeen", who refused to worship idols and searched for God in creeds other than those of their fathers and forefathers.

Gary Dale: *Were there many other Christians in Arabia at the time?*

Dr. Mustafa: No evidence exists in history that proves that there was a big Christian community in Mecca and Waraqah was not a Bishop of Mecca. The explanation for that was that Mecca was an important commercial center in the Arabian Peninsula, in whose worship, rituals and trade, many tribes which were living in the Peninsula were united. Each tribe preserved its worship, rituals and gods and sent samples to the noblest of places in Mecca, Al-Kaaba, in which were preserved samples of the gods of Arab tribes. Special festive seasons were devoted there to perform pilgrimage and visit these gods. Therefore, it was no coincidence that the political and trade leadership in Mecca fiercely opposed the new call of Islam. When they could not overcome it, they joined it.

Gary Dale: *The Chick Publication in question claims that Waraqah had a great deal of influence in Mohammed's theological development. Can you briefly address this?*

Dr. Mustafa: We sometimes read in several historical sources of Christian inclination to exaggeration, in my opinion, of the role played by Waraqah in the formation of the Islamic creed of Mohammed. Doubtless, Mohammed was influenced by the teachings of both Judaism and Christianity. Islam considers itself a continuation and completion of the two religions. Historical Muslim sources prove Waraqah ibn Nawfal's welcoming of Mohammed's prophet hood. However, anyone who is deeply knowledgeable about the Islamic teachings notices differences between Islam and the other two religions as there were differences between Christ's teachings and those of Judaism. Prophet Mohammed lived in a different age and environment and was distinguished by genius that qualified him to bring new things too. Had Waraqah been the mentor and revelation for Mohammed, why didn't he himself call for it, as he had a status, reputation and roots that were not unequal to Mohammed's.

Gary Dale: *It seems to me far fetched that Waraqah would have even been able to have had anything to do with the Catholic Church as Alberto Rivera claims in his tale of conspiracy. No one knows for certain what brand of Christianity Waraqah followed. Could you possibly shed any light on the matter?*

<u>Dr. Mustafa:</u> Waraqah lived in the second half of the 6th century and beginning of the 7th century AD. He adopted Christianity at the hands of religious men in Damascus. The Damascene Church was attached to Constantinople, or the Eastern Church. Therefore, I think it is unlikely that Waraqah was a Catholic. Moreover, I agree with you that talking about Islam as if it were a Catholic conspiracy for the control of Jerusalem is far-fetched and daring fantasy of interpreting history, which is the result of economic, social and political conditions and not the result of conspiracy.

<u>Gary Dale:</u> *So whether Waraqah was theologically a Nestorian who followed one of the Oriental Church traditions that Catholics consider heresy, as were many of the Christians in Arabia, or since Waraqah was converted to Christianity in Damascus he followed an early version of what would have become the Eastern Orthodox tradition which would have been looking to Constantinople, which you seem to believe to also be somewhat probable, I think we do agree that it was extremely highly unlikely that Waraqah was a Roman Catholic, let alone serving as a monk and agent of the Roman Catholic Church. Now let's look at the claims near the end of Alberto Rivera's story where he says that the miracles witnessed in Fátima, Portugal, were all aimed at getting Arabs to convert to Catholicism. Rivera followed this up with a quote or paraphrase from Archbishop Fulton J. Sheen which I have not been able to fully verify. In my text I*

have laid out several reasons why none of this could be true. But let's entertain the idea that this part of Alberto Rivera's was actually true. I still don't see any Arabs converting to Catholicism. Can you offer a few words on this subject?

Dr. Mustafa: I think that the present phase of relationship between religions in the world, especially the three monotheistic religions, is characterized by the awareness and conviction of the followers of each of these three religions of their beliefs. The relationship that connects the followers of these religions is tolerance, recognition of the other and respect for the differences among them. Therefore, I think that conversion is rare and if it occurs, there would be narrow material interests behind it. Religion in the Arab world constitutes an essential component of the social fabric and it has deep impact on customs and traditions. It is also part of the essence of human activities, such as marriage, holiday observance, occasions and others. Consequently, conversion is not easy. And if it happens, it leads to the isolation and distancing of the converter from his family and group. On the basis of my general observations, I don't see a conversion movement. Even moving from one sect to another is rare for the same reasons, e.g., a Sunni becomes a Shiite or an Orthodox to Catholic. Moving to a sect may occur in order to get support or financial or educational assistance and not more.

How the Vatican Created Islam

Below is the text from Jack Chick's book regarding Alberto Rivera's claims. Although this is an abbreviated form, it is taken directly from Jack Chick's comic book, The Prophet, by Jack T. Chick, Chick Publications, 1988. The words below have appeared on hundred's of websites, from religious sites, to neo-Nazi sites to conspiracy theory sites. The site that I have seen pop up through the most sources is from the conspiracy theorist David Icke and has been posted at:

http://www.davidicke.com/content/view/746/59/

It is this text below that I have used for my analysis in this book because I believe many more have seen this rendition than have actually read the comic book itself. I received this by e-mail from people I knew New Zealand, the United States and Malaysia before I read it fully. Since then I have received this from more people in other countries, some of whom I did not even know.

It is interesting to note that the website that David Icke uses as his second source is a dead site. The first one is from another conspiracy theory site.

If you note the introduction, this does not even mention that the publisher, Chick Publications, is neither a religious tract publisher nor that Alberto Rivera is a very controversial figure. This actually looks like a ground breaking revelation due to the words "astonishing story" and "His testimony should not be silenced."

Herein is the danger of the propaganda. To make the untrue appear to be a hidden truth. To make the real truth appear to be a façade that we are all shaded with. And to spread just enough of the familiar in the lie that one might bite it hook line and sinker if one is simply too lazy to dig deeper and find the read truth.

In my opinion, Jack Chick and Alberto Rivera have a lot to answer for.

The Text:

Thursday, 13 April 2006

'How the Vatican created Islam'

Source: http://www.cloakanddagger.de/lenny/alberto_rivera.htm

How the Vatican created Islam. The astonishing story from an ex-Jesuit priest, Alberto Rivera, which was told to him by Cardinal Bea while he was at the Vatican.

From "The Prophet":

http://www.choosinglife.net/Islam.htm

This information came from Alberto Rivera, former Jesuit priest after his conversion to Protestant Christianity. It is excerpted from "The

Prophet," published by Chick Publications, PO Box 662, Chino CA 91708. Since its publication, after several unsuccessful attempts on his life, he died suddenly from food poisoning. His testimony should not be silenced. Dr. Rivera speaks to us still...

"What I'm going to tell you is what I learned in secret briefings in the Vatican when I was a Jesuit priest, under oath and induction. A Jesuit cardinal named Augustine Bea showed us how desperately the Roman Catholics wanted Jerusalem at the end of the third century. Because of its religious history and its strategic location, the Holy City was considered a priceless treasure. A scheme had to be developed to make Jerusalem a Roman Catholic city.

"The great untapped source of manpower that could do this job was the children of Ishmael. The poor Arabs fell victim to one of the most clever plans ever devised by the powers of darkness. Early Christians went everywhere with the gospel setting up small churches, but they met heavy opposition. Both the Jews and the Roman government persecuted the believers in Christ to stop their spread. But the Jews rebelled against Rome, and in 70 AD, Roman armies under General Titus smashed Jerusalem and destroyed the great Jewish temple which was the heart of Jewish worship...in fulfillment of Christ's prophecy in Matthew 24:2.

"On this holy placed today where the temple once stood, the Dome of the Rock Mosque stands as Islam's second most holy place. Sweeping changes were in the wind. Corruption, apathy, greed, cruelty, perversion and rebellion were eating at the Roman Empire, and it was ready to collapse. The persecution against Christians was useless as they continued to lay down their lives for the gospel of Christ.

"The only way Satan could stop this thrust was to create a counterfeit "Christian" religion to destroy the work of God. The solution was in Rome. Their religion had come from ancient Babylon and all it needed was a face-lift. This didn't happen overnight, but began in the writings of the 'early church fathers'.

"It was through their writings that a new religion would take shape. The statue of Jupiter in Rome was eventually called St. Peter, and the statue of Venus was changed to the Virgin Mary. The site chosen for its headquarters was on one of the seven hills called 'Vaticanus', the place of the diving serpent where the Satanic temple of Janus stood.

"The great counterfeit religion was Roman Catholicism, called 'Mystery, Babylon the Great, the Mother of Harlots and Abominations of the Earth'- Revelation 17:5. She was raised up to block the gospel, slaughter the believers in Christ, establish religions, create wars and make the nations drunk with the wine of her fornication as we will see.

"Three major religions have one thing in common - each has a holy place where they look for guidance. Roman Catholicism looks to the Vatican as the Holy City. The Jews look to the wailing wall in Jerusalem, and the Muslims look to Mecca as their Holy City. Each group believes that they receive certain types of blessings for the rest of their lives for visiting their holy place. In the beginning, Arab visitors would bring gifts to the 'House of God', and the keepers of the Kaaba were gracious to all who came. Some brought their idols and, not wanting to offend these people, their idols were placed inside the sanctuary. It is said that the Jews looked upon the Kaaba as an outlying tabernacle of the Lord with veneration until it became polluted with idols.

"In a tribal contention over a well (Zamzam) the treasure of the Kaaba and the offerings that pilgrims had given were dumped down the well and it was filled with sand - it disappeared. Many years later Adb Al-Muttalib was given visions telling him where to find the well and its treasure. He became the hero of Mecca, and he was destined to become the grandfather of Muhammad. Before this time, Augustine became the bishop of North Africa and was effective in winning Arabs to Roman Catholicism, including whole tribes. It was among these Arab converts to Catholicism that the concept of looking for an Arab prophet developed.

"Muhammad's father died from illness and sons born to great Arab families in places like Mecca were sent into the desert to be suckled and weaned and spend some of their childhood with Bedouin tribes for training and to avoid the plagues in the cities.

"After his mother and grandfather also died, Muhammad was with his uncle when a Roman Catholic monk learned of his identity and said,

"Take your brother's son back to his country and guard him against the Jews, for by god, if they see him and know of him that which I know, they will construe evil against him. Great things are in store for this brother's son of yours."

"The Roman Catholic monk had fanned the flames for future Jewish persecutions at the hands of the followers of Muhammad. The Vatican desperately wanted Jerusalem because of its religious significance, but was blocked by the Jews.

"Another problem was the true Christians in North Africa who preached the gospel. Roman Catholicism was growing in power, but would not tolerate opposition. Somehow the Vatican had to create a weapon to eliminate both the Jews and the true Christian believers who refused to accept Roman Catholicism. Looking to North Africa, they saw the multitudes of Arabs as a source of manpower to do their dirty work. Some Arabs had become Roman Catholic, and could be used in reporting information to leaders in Rome. Others were used in an underground spy network to carry out Rome's master plan to control the great multitudes of Arabs who rejected Catholicism. When 'St Augustine' appeared on the scene, he knew what was going on. His monasteries served as bases to seek out and destroy Bible manuscripts owned by the true Christians.

"The Vatican wanted to create a messiah for the Arabs, someone they could raise up as a great leader, a man with charisma whom they could train, and eventually unite all the non-Catholic Arabs behind him, creating a mighty army that would ultimately capture Jerusalem for the pope. In the Vatican briefing, Cardinal Bea told us this story:

'A wealthy Arabian lady who was a faithful follower of the pope played a tremendous part in this drama. She was a widow named Khadijah. She gave her wealth to the church and retired to a convent, but was given an assignment. She was to find a brilliant young man who could be used by the Vatican to create a new religion and become the messiah for the children of Ishmael. Khadijah had a cousin named Waraquah,, who was also a very faithful Roman Catholic and the Vatican placed him in a critical role as Muhammad's advisor. He had tremendous influence on Muhammad.

'Teachers were sent to young Muhammad and he had intensive training. Muhammad studied the works of St. Augustine which prepared him for his "great calling." The Vatican had Catholic Arabs across North Africa spread the story of a great one who was about to rise up among the people and be the chosen one of their God.

'While Muhammad was being prepared, he was told that his enemies were the Jews and that the only true Christians were Roman Catholic. He was taught that others calling themselves Christians were actually wicked impostors and should be destroyed. Many Muslims believe this.

'Muhammad began receiving "divine revelations" and his wife's Catholic cousin Waraquah helped interpret them. From this came the

184

Koran. In the fifth year of Muhammad's mission, persecution came against his followers because they refused to worship the idols in the Kaaba.

'Muhammad instructed some of them to flee to Abysinnia where Negus, the Roman Catholic king accepted them because Muhammad's views on the virgin Mary were so close to Roman Catholic doctrine. These Muslims received protection from Catholic kings because of Muhammad's revelations.

'Muhammad later conquered Mecca and the Kaaba was cleared of idols. History proves that before Islam came into existence, the Sabeans in Arabia worshiped the moon-god who was married to the sun-god. They gave birth to three goddesses who were worshipped throughout the Arab world as "Daughters of Allah" An idol excavated at Hazor in Palestine in 1950's shows Allah sitting on a throne with the crescent moon on his chest.

'Muhammad claimed he had a vision from Allah and was told, "You are the messenger of Allah." This began his career as a prophet and he received many messages. By the time Muhammad died, the religion of Islam was exploding. The nomadic Arab tribes were joining forces in the name of Allah and his prophet, Muhammad.

'Some of Muhammad's writings were placed in the Koran, others were never published. They are now in the hands of high ranking holy men (Ayatollahs) in the Islamic faith.'

"When Cardinal Bea shared with us in the Vatican, he said, these writings are guarded because they contain information that links the Vatican to the creation of Islam. Both sides have so much information on each other, that if exposed, it could create such a scandal that it would be a disaster for both religions.

"In their "holy" book, the Koran, Christ is regarded as only a prophet. If the pope was His representative on earth, then he also must be a prophet of God. This caused the followers of Muhammad to fear and respect the pope as another "holy man."

"The pope moved quickly and issued bulls granting the Arab generals permission to invade and conquer the nations of North Africa. The Vatican helped to finance the building of these massive Islamic armies in exchange for three favors:

1. Eliminate the Jews and Christians (true believers, which they called infidels).

2. Protect the Augustinian Monks and Roman Catholics.

3. Conquer Jerusalem for "His Holiness" in the Vatican.

"As time went by, the power of Islam became tremendous - Jews and true Christians were slaughtered, and Jerusalem fell into their hands. Roman Catholics were never attacked, nor were their shrines, during this time. But when the pope asked for Jerusalem, he was surprised at their denial! The Arab generals had such military success that they could not be intimidated by the pope - nothing could stand in the way of their own plan.

"Under Waraquah's direction, Muhammad wrote that Abraham offered Ishmael as a sacrifice. The Bible says that Isaac was the sacrifice, but Muhammad removed Isaac's name and inserted Ishmael's name. As a result of this and Muhammad's vision, the faithful Muslims built a mosque, the Dome of the Rock, in Ishmael's honor on the site of the Jewish temple that was destroyed in 70 AD. This made Jerusalem the 2nd most holy place in the Islam faith. How could they give such a sacred shrine to the pope without causing a revolt?

"The pope realized what they had created was out of control when he heard they were calling "His Holiness" an infidel. The Muslim generals were determined to conquer the world for Allah and now they turned toward Europe. Islamic ambassadors approached the pope and asked for papal bulls to give them permission to invade European countries.

"The Vatican was outraged; war was inevitable. Temporal power and control of the world was considered the basic right of the pope. He wouldn't think of sharing it with those whom he considered heathens.

"The pope raised up his armies and called them crusades to hold back the children of Ishmael from grabbing Catholic Europe. The crusades lasted centuries and Jerusalem slipped out of the pope's hands.

"Turkey fell and Spain and Portugal were invaded by Islamic forces. In Portugal, they called a mountain village "Fatima" in honor of Muhammad's daughter, never dreaming it would become world famous.

"Years later when the Muslim armies were poised on the islands of Sardinia and Corsica, to invade Italy, there was a serious problem. The Islamic generals realized they were too far extended. It was time for peace talks. One of the negotiators was Francis of Assisi.

"As a result, the Muslims were allowed to occupy Turkey in a "Christian" world, and the Catholics were allowed to occupy Lebanon in the Arab world. It was also agreed that the Muslims could build mosques in Catholic countries without interference as long as Roman Catholicism could flourish Arab countries.

"Cardinal Bea told us in Vatican briefings that both the Muslims and Roman Catholics agreed to block and destroy the efforts of their common enemy, Bible-believing Christian missionaries. Through these concordats, Satan blocked the children of Ishmael from a knowledge of Scripture and the truth.

"A light control was kept on Muslims from the Ayatollah down through the Islamic priests, nuns and monks. The Vatican also engineers a campaign of hatred between the Muslim Arabs and the Jews. Before this, they had co-existed peacefully.

"The Islamic community looks on the Bible-believing missionary as a devil who brings poison to the children of Allah. This explains years of ministry in those countries with little results.

"The next plan was to control Islam. In 1910, Portugal was going Socialistic. Red flags were appearing and the Catholic Church was facing a major problem. Increasing numbers were against the church.

"The Jesuits wanted Russia involved, and the location of this vision at Fatima could play a key part in pulling Islam to the Mother Church.

"In 1917, the Virgin appeared in Fatima. "The Mother of God" was a smashing success, playing to overflow crowds. As a result, the Socialists of Portugal suffered a major defeat.

"Roman Catholics world-wide began praying for the conversion of Russia and the Jesuits invented the Novenas to Fatima which they could perform throughout North Africa, spreading good public relations to the Muslim world. The Arabs thought they were honoring the daughter of Muhammad, which is what the Jesuits wanted them to believe.

"As a result of the vision of Fatima, Pope Pius XII ordered his Nazi army to crush Russia and the Orthodox religion and make Russia Roman Catholic." A few years after he lost World War II, Pope Pius XII startled the world with his phoney dancing sun vision to keep Fatima in the news. It was great religious show biz and the world swallowed it.

"Not surprisingly, Pope Pius was the only one to see this vision. As a result, a group of followers has grown into a Blue Army world-wide, totaling millions of faithful Roman Catholics ready to die for the blessed virgin.

"But we haven't seen anything yet. The Jesuits have their Virgin Mary scheduled to appear four or five times in China, Russia, and major appearance in the U.S.

"What has this got to do with Islam? Note Bishop Sheen's statement: "Our Lady's appearances at Fatima marked the turning point in the history of the world's 350 million Muslims. After the death of his daughter, Muhammad wrote that she "is the most holy of all women in Paradise, next to Mary."

"He believed that the Virgin Mary chose to be known as Our Lady of Fatima as a sign and a pledge that the Muslims who believe in Christ's virgin birth, will come to believe in His divinity.

"Bishop Sheen pointed out that the pilgrim virgin statues of Our Lady of Fatima were enthusiastically received by Muslims in Africa, India, and elsewhere, and that many Muslims are now coming into the Roman Catholic Church."

Acknowledgements

I would like to start by thanking my lovely mother, Bobbie Cordelia Blevins, who did the hard yards to get me grown. I wasn't easy then and I guess I am still not. I love her for it and there is not a day that passes that I don't remember how much I love my mother.

To Billy Bob and Elva Smith, thanks for being the backbone of the clan for all of these years. You have given me the anchor in life that is called heritage and I love you both for it.

I want to show my gratitude for the various people who graciously let me interview them for their expertise. These kind people are from all walks of life and from varied religious backgrounds. Without them this book would not have been nearly as rich!

My thanks to: Deacon George Kozak, Kurt Kuersteiner, Ralph Williams, Len Rosen, Father Felix Al-Shabi, Dr. Walid Mustafa, Imam Dr. Yusuf Ziya Kavakci and N.S. Dill for their expert help and guidance in getting the research for this book done.

I also would like to name some of the teachers in my life who over the decades have made lasting and deep impressions on me:

Sharon (Lassiter) Bard, Annie Pearl Bailey, Ned Duncan, Wanda Haney, Virginia Duke, Cheryl Ann McDonald, James Gober, Doyle

Malcom, Jane Purtle, Betty Stinson, Johnnie Hamilton, Jr., Wanda Fincher and Steve Warnock.

I never thought I would name Ted Kirby to such a list because of the times he would take me to task. But the older I got I certainly see how the tables have turned. He put up with lots of unnecessary monkey business and I can now say I can see where he was coming from.

(Thank you Mr. Kirby!)

I thank my big sister Diana Caye Cearley for all the love and support she has shown me through the years. I couldn't have been without Donna Graham and Jan Rhodes either.

Gary Lyons is another person who is somewhere in the past. I knew that moved to Hawaii maybe twenty-five years ago or more to do work for the Churches of Christ. He may not know it but he was most likely the one who stoked my interest in the history and culture that was to be found in the Bible.

Brother Gene Cloer was the man who drove home the necessity to be sure about what you are reading, seeing and hearing when it comes to the truth.

I have two special thank yous now at the end:

To Harvey Harris Blevins, Nubbin… Thank you for being yourself. You taught me many of life's lessons and still do. You have taught by words and by example. You are a rock and I am proud to call you family.

To Harvey Dale Saunders Cearley… Thank you, Son, for reminding me how much I loved books when I was your age! Here's to hoping that your budding love affair with knowledge will only grow.

Gary Dale Cearley

About the Author…

Gary Dale Cearley was born on March 5th, 1967, and raised about ten miles outside of Prescott, Arkansas. He went into the United States Navy two months after graduating Prescott High School graduating boot camp at the Recruit Training Center in San Diego, California. Later he received language training in Vietnamese at the Defense Language Institute in Monterey, California and further military training at Goodfellow Air Force Base in San Angelo, Texas. Ironically, after Goodfellow Air Force Base Gary Dale received orders to the USS Arkansas, his home state's name sake vessel.

After the leaving the United States Navy, Gary Dale went to work in Los Angeles, living in the Venice Beach area. He began a career in international shipping and freight forwarding. But as Gary Dale had longed to see the world for all of his life he went with his first wife, Maureen Luna-Long, to work in Seoul, Republic of Korea. Later on the opportunity to work in Vietnam presented itself and he has been living there ever since.

Gary Dale is an avid libertarian who founded the organization Libertarians Abroad on July 4th, 2005. He has been a member and supporter of the national Libertarian Party since his days in the Navy when a shipmate loaned him the Lysander Spooner tract _No Treason_. He has also been very active in developing the sport of darts in Vietnam. Gary Dale was chairman of the Hanoi International Darts

League prior to moving to Ho Chi Minh City where he got the Saigon International Darts League its first season. He was the first chairman of the league in Saigon and is still actively involved, serving as the vice chairman of the league today. Notable achievements have included organizing Vietnam's very first international darts competition in August of 2005 which was attended by a team from Singapore. The Vietnam side won!

Gary Dale is a graduate of the Defense Language Institute in Monterey, California, and is fluent in three dialects of Vietnamese. He also speaks several other languages as well. Gary Dale worked my way through my education by night school, challenge exams, etc., also graduated the University of the State of New York with an Associate of Science degree in Liberal Arts and a Bachelor of Science degree in Sociology. Later Gary Dale also completed a Master of Public Administration degree at the University of Oklahoma, but he says that he will always be a Razorback!

Made in the USA
San Bernardino, CA
06 August 2020